**VITO ACCONCI** ACCONCI STUDIO

Vito Acconci. *Houses up the Wall*, 1985.
Stained wood, vinyl, mirrored Plexiglas, plants.
10 x 16 x 4 ½ ft.

**VITO ACCONCI**  ACCONCI STUDIO

# ACTS OF ARCHITECTURE

Curated by

DEAN SOBEL AND MARGARET ANDERA

With contributions by

DEAN SOBEL

SANFORD KWINTER

VITO ACCONCI

MILWAUKEE ART MUSEUM

# Acconci Studio 1988–2001

Luis Vera

Jenny Schrider

Darío Nuñez

Celia Imrey

Sergio Prego

Brownie Johnson

Matthew Pickner

Charles Doherty

Peter Dorsey

Stephen Roe

Azarakhsh Damood

Renee Piechocki

Ron Ervolino

Kyle Steinfeld

Saija Singer

Rafael Varela

Thomas King

Suchitra Van

Sean Weiss

Bevin Savage

Sara Peschel

Nanna Wulfing

Simone Steinlechner

Katrin Pesch

Anthony Arnold

Young-Eun Choi

Tako Reyenga

Martin Knussel

Arnaud Schroeder

Jan Theissen

Wo Chang

Lisa Albin

Alison Grossman

Serena Heres

Paula Young

Sarah Krasley

John Cleater

Jeff Smith

Mark Trautrimas

Andrea Claire

Jennifer Zackin

Monica Hudson

Jorge Prado

Silva Ajemian

# Contents

Vito Acconci. *Sub-Urb,* 1983. Stained and painted wood,
steel, Astroturf. 10 x 21 x 98 ft.

# Foreword

RUSSELL BOWMAN
Director

The Milwaukee Art Museum is pleased to present this traveling exhibition of the work of Vito Acconci and Acconci Studio. The present exhibition focuses on the artist's work since 1980. This aspect of Acconci's extraordinary and influential career has never been examined in an American museum exhibition. Over the past twenty years Acconci's art has become more elaborate and taken on very different forms, including sculptures that double as furniture and "self-erecting architectural units," in which viewer participation is an essential component of the work. Since the 1990s he has sought to reach an even broader audience by designing public works—such as playgrounds, gardens, and parks—and by working with architects to create projects that are integrated into buildings and plazas.

This exhibition was initially developed by Dean Sobel while he was chief curator and curator of contemporary art at the Milwaukee Art Museum, and it continued under his leadership after he became director of the Aspen Art Museum. Dean's commitment to see this exhibition through to its completion during a career transition speaks to his dedication to this project. It was a pleasure to work with him again.

This publication would not have been possible without the generous support of Camille O. Hoffmann. The exhibition was supported in part by a grant from the National Endowment for the Arts, a federal agency. I would also like to thank Marti Mayo, director, Contemporary Arts Museum, Houston, and Suzanne Delahanty, director, Miami Art Museum, and their staffs for their participation in the exhibition tour.

Vito Acconci. *Maze Table*, 1985.
Glass. 30 x 144 x 144 in.

# Acknowledgments

DEAN SOBEL
Guest Curator

The genesis of this exhibition can be traced back to 1996, when, as curator of contemporary art at the Milwaukee Art Museum, I was asked to serve on the selection committee to choose artists to create public artworks for the Midwest Express Center in Milwaukee. Our committee unanimously chose Vito Acconci and the Acconci Studio to work with the project's design/build team to create an integrated work for the center. This decision led not only to the creation of *Walkways through the Wall* (1998, see page 38), which is documented in this exhibition, but also to the first discussions between Acconci, myself, and the Milwaukee Art Museum about a (perhaps overdue) exhibition of his work of the 1980s and 1990s. It is a great pleasure to see this exhibition and publication fully realized now, five years later.

There are a number of individuals whose efforts were essential to this undertaking. I would first like to acknowledge the substantial contributions made by Margaret Andera, assistant curator at the Milwaukee Art Museum, who not only managed the project in Milwaukee but was also my close collaborator. We would both like to thank Sean Weiss of the Acconci Studio, who proved indispensable to virtually every aspect of the exhibition and catalogue.

On behalf of the Milwaukee Art Museum, I would also like to extend my gratitude to the institutional and private lenders, who generously parted with their works so they could be part of this exhibition and tour. Acconci's representatives—including Barbara Gladstone, Ivy Shapiro, and Mark Hughes of the Barbara Gladstone Gallery, New York, and Rhona Hoffman of Rhona Hoffman Gallery, Chicago—were instrumental in securing essential loans. John Tagiuri, engineer for many of Acconci's works of the 1980s, was re-enlisted for this exhibition, ensuring the proper installation of the artist's often complicated works.

It has been a great pleasure to work again with my friends and colleagues at the Milwaukee Art Museum. I am especially grateful to Russell Bowman, director, who has enthusiastically supported this project since its inception. Brian Ferriso, senior director of curatorial affairs, oversaw the key areas of budget, contracts, and staffing. I am grateful for his involvement. Julia Jackson, curatorial department intern, compiled the artist's lengthy exhibition history, bibliography, and listing of public projects. Leigh Albritton, registrar, arranged for the packing and shipment of the works with great skill and care. Steve Biel, director of design and publications, was responsible for the design of this handsome publication. Lucia Petrie, director of development, led the grant-writing and fund-raising process, and Eva Berry, communications coordinator, handled the public relations duties.

Sanford Kwinter, associate professor of architecture at Rice University in Houston, contributed an insightful essay to this publication. Karen Jacobson edited the various texts and also provided valuable counsel regarding the organization of this book.

Finally, I would like to thank Vito Acconci for his deep commitment to this project. His involvement in every aspect of this exhibition has resulted in one that more fully expresses the sum and substance of this multifaceted artist. It is enormously gratifying to see this exhibition come to fruition.

# Introduction

DEAN SOBEL

In 1980, after spending nearly two decades as a concrete poet, photo-conceptualist, videographer, and installation artist, Vito Acconci set out on a new artistic path that he has continued to follow to this day. Extending many of the notions he had been developing and refining in the 1960s and 1970s, Acconci began designing sculptures patterned after architectural and furniture forms as well as unique variations of public art. Viewer interaction was essential to these works, particularly his "self-erecting architectural units," which required a participant to "complete" them, and his outdoor projects, which became part of the world at large.

Because of the absolutely legendary status Acconci attained early in his career—his provocative body and performance works of the late 1960s and early 1970s were among the most discussed and influential artistic activities of that highly exploratory era—his more recent endeavors have been somewhat overshadowed. This has been especially true in the United States, where, during the 1980s, his new work has been presented in relatively small portions and, over the past ten years, hardly at all.[1] In 1988 the Museum of Modern Art presented a selection of Acconci's earliest house and furniture works, examples of which were also included in the last full-scale Acconci survey in the United States, a relatively modest presentation of works from 1967 to 1987, which traveled only to small venues during 1987 and 1988.[2] Since the time of these exhibitions, however, Acconci has continued to elaborate on these sculptural forms, and his career has developed in important and perhaps unexpected ways.

The methods and forms Acconci used in his work of the 1980s anticipated a number of approaches to art making that have gained widespread acceptance today. His deliberate movement away from self-referential artistic activities (such as solo performances) toward discrete (and, for this artist, more traditional) sculptural forms redolent with sociopolitical commentary links him to a generation of younger artists, such as Robert Gober, Rachel Whiteread, and Janine Antoni. Acconci's dissatisfaction with overly hermetic activities is also apparent in his decision to work as part of a collaborative team (he now considers himself part of a studio—the Acconci Studio—rather than an independent artist). This rejection of the modernist notion of the autonomous artist is shared by many younger artists, who, to accommodate increasingly ambitious projects, have likewise embraced a team approach. Among the most significant examples are Jeff Koons and Takashi Murakami, who have employed as many as thirty craftsmen for the production of their paintings and sculptures, and Matthew Barney, whose feature-length films have involved entire film crews.

During the 1980s Acconci also dismantled and merged various stylistic and functional categories in works that straddled the boundaries of sculpture, furniture, design, and architecture. In essence he created a new art form, which, at that point, was entirely his own. This approach, which many have identified as emblematic of so-called postmodernism, has now become commonplace among young artists all over the world. The influence of Acconci's furniture-cum-sculpture—works such as *Head Storage* (1985) or the Multi-Bed series (1991)—is detectable in the work of artists such as Liam Gillick, Joep van Lieshout, Thomas Locher, Jorge Pardo, and Tobias Rehberger, all of whom borrow strategies from the fields of design and architecture. Andrea Zittel's miniature "living units" find their antecedents in Acconci's "portable architecture," including works such as *Storage Unit for People and Things* (1984) and his slightly later *Mobile Linear City* (1991). Acconci's perverse manipulations of architecture and public art—seen in *Bad Dream House* (1984) and *Floor Clock* (1989)—are also quite relevant in light of Gregor Schneider's nightmarish room installations and Gabriel Orozco's semi-subterranean Ferris wheel.[3] It appears that Acconci, quite unknowingly, swung the doors wide open for many of today's most promising younger artists.

In the 1990s Acconci produced some of the strongest works of his long career, such as *Convertible Clam Shelter* (1990) and *Adjustable Wall Bra* (1990–91), which are icons of late twentieth-century art. However, since 1990 he has deliberately devoted most of his energies to architectural projects. By collaborating with a team of architects and project managers, he has moved outside the gallery and away from the mainstream of the art world. (The public works are represented in this exhibition through models displayed in a system specially designed by the Acconci Studio.) These large-scale projects constitute an important body of work that, in many respects, can be seen as a logical continuation of his artistic trajectory. This exhibition and publication provide the first major examination of the "second half" of Acconci's career, a period characterized by works that are, in their own fashion, every bit as startling, provocative, and influential as those of his "classic" period of the 1960s and 1970s.

Acconci Studio (Vito Acconci, Celia Imrey, Darío Nuñez, Saija Singer). *Tele-Furni-System*, 1997.
Multichannel video installation with monitors, speakers, steel and pipe armature.
Dimensions variable (approx. 192 x 240 x 276 in.).

## NOTES

**1** Many of Acconci's U.S. exhibitions since the mid-1990s have concentrated on his work of the 1960s and 1970s (for example, the solo exhibition at Barbara Gladstone Gallery, New York, in 1997 and *Vito Acconci: Performance Documentation and Photoworks, 1969– 1973*, Ubu Gallery, New York, 2001).

**2** *Vito Acconci: Public Places* was presented at the Museum of Modern Art in New York from February 11 to May 3, 1988. *Vito Acconci: Domestic Trappings*, organized by the La Jolla Museum of Contemporary Art, traveled to the Neuberger Museum of Art, Purchase, New York; the Aspen Art Museum, Colorado; and Laumeier Sculpture Park, Saint Louis, between June 1987 and June 1988.

**3** Orozco realized the Ferris wheel project for Expo 2000 in Hannover but first proposed it in 1997; see Klaus Bussmann, Kasper König, and Florian Matzner, eds., *Contemporary Sculpture: Projects in Münster, 1997* (Stuttgart: Gerd Hatje, 1997), 296–99.

Acconci Studio (Vito Acconci,
Luis Vera, Jenny Schrider, Lisa Albin).
*Personal Island*, 1992.
Zoetermeer, Netherlands.
Aluminum rowboats, steel, dirt,
grass, and trees. 10 x 12 x 36 ft.

# FROM THOUGHT TO MONUMENT

## Vito Acconci's Art of the 1980s and 1990s

DEAN SOBEL

Throughout his multivalent career, which now extends over five decades, Vito Acconci has always connected his activities to reality: real thoughts, real places, real time, real experiences. Consequently he has become a master at eliciting direct, oftentimes visceral responses (whether physical, emotional, or intellectual) from his viewers. In fact, perhaps no other artist has been so ardently concerned with the position of the viewer within the nexus of art making and presentation. Over time, however, his approach to the viewer has changed, and so have the forms he has chosen for his artworks.

Acconci's early performance, video, and sound works were intended to arouse genuine feelings in audience members—such as fear, confusion, or even boredom—by luring them into uncertain or even dangerous situations. In these early works the artist's persona was always at the forefront, represented either through video or through photographic images, recordings of his voice, or through his actual presence. In his works since 1980—which have taken more concrete forms, patterned after sculpture, furniture, architecture, and other three-dimensional media—he has coaxed his viewers to be part of the art in more polite ways. He has also allowed himself to recede into the background, keeping the aura of the artist in line with the other issues he is interested in exploring. In these works Acconci has found a more balanced relationship between artist, spectator, and object.

Acconci's desire to establish a relationship with his audience is evident in his earliest creative activities. His involvement with literature and poetry in the mid-1960s, first as a student at the University of Iowa, then as an active member of the poetry scene in New York, was the starting point. Using words on a printed page in what he later called "language pieces," he forged a dialogue, whether with a reader or with the audiences at his readings. In an untitled poem from 1968, Acconci, in the first person, describes actions of his body:

Now I will tell you the truth. I am nodding my head.
Now I will you something that cannot be questioned.
I am waving my hands.
Now I will tell you the facts. I am moving my legs.[2]

Vito Acconci. *Seedbed,* 1972.
Sonnabend Gallery, New York.
Performance/installation.
Nine days, eight hours a day,
during a three-week exhibition.

Acconci engaged his readers by drawing them into a game of separating fact from fiction. By referring to his own body, he placed himself at the center of what he is describing. He has referred to the relationship between voice, text, and reader as a "model space, a performance area in miniature."[3] This space would become one of artist, object, and viewer in his later art.

Between 1969 and 1971 Acconci turned to "performance situations" in an attempt to root in real time the kinds of thoughts and actions he was describing in his texts. In various private performances—such as his classic "body" works, in which he marked, bit, manipulated, or involved his body in other ways—he was attempting to understand the physicality of his being. In performances that involved the environment, a participant, or an audience, he conceptualized his relationship to the world at large. For Acconci, each individual commands part of a "region"; in his early performance works, he wanted these regions to collide.[4]

As Acconci moved his activities into more conventional gallery settings, he was able to frame his interaction with his audience more precisely. In his notorious *Seedbed* installation of 1972, he masturbated beneath a gently sloping floor while viewers entered the otherwise generic gallery setting above. He addressed them through a sound system. They could hear and feel his presence, but his body went unseen. Unknowingly each visitor entered into a private relationship with the artist in an otherwise public space. The result, for many, was a feeling of confusion and transgression.

Later in the 1970s Acconci made fuller use of the gallery space in larger and more sculpturally complex installations. Employing written texts, sound elements, videotaped images, slide projections, lighting, and props, he engineered spaces in which viewers moved through various stages of involvement and meaning. In *Leveling*, one of his most complex installations of the mid-1970s, he used the gallery as a narrative device by assigning a different category of nouns (persons, places, things) to each of three separate rooms. Like many of his works of this period, this installation explored systems of knowledge, thought, and organization.

During the late 1970s Acconci made the significant decision to broaden the artist-viewer relationship into one of artist and community. Viewers were asked to consider their connection not only to the artist but to a larger group as well. These works are the genesis of his projects of the 1980s. In *Middle of the World* (1976), a wooden platform was both suspended from a gallery balcony and tethered to the floor by makeshift rope ladders. A single audio speaker broadcast a stream of voices, each seemingly attempting to establish its own ideological "platform." The dynamics of group interaction were also implied in *Where We Are Now (Who Are We Anyway?)*, a 1976 installation consisting of eight pairs of stools lined up along a long wooden table that extended out a third-story window. An audio track posed questions to invisible characters seated at the table, challenging them to draw conclusions:

Vito Acconci.
*Where We Are Now
(Who Are We Anyway)*, 1976.
Wooden tables, stools,
painted walls with audio.
10 x 30 x 70 ft.

> Now that we know we failed…
> And what do you think, Rita?
> Now that we do what we can…
> And what do you think, Martin?
> Now that we do what we have to…
> And what do you think, Julia?[5]

The futility of group decision-making is made apparent by the characters' blank answers and by the way the table extends out the window, like a hangman's plank.

Like many artists active during the mid-1970s—a period marked by the unsatisfying conclusion of the Vietnam War, a climate of political mistrust engendered by Watergate, troubles in the Middle East, the rise of the feminist movement, and a faltering U.S. economy, all complicated by the commemoration of America's bicentennial in 1976—Acconci's art began to reveal more specific sociopolitical themes. *The Red Tapes* (1976), his last video work, and two related installations, *The American Gift* (1976) and *Another Candy Bar from G.I. Joe* (1977), collectively refer to American hegemony, the bomb, imperialism, and male power. The two installations—created for exhibitions in France and Italy, respectively—included audiotapes of Acconci's voice (reciting nationalistic propaganda) as a way to represent the authoritative voice of American power. He concluded the 1970s with several installations that featured high-tension wires, precarious tetherings, and contraptions that harnessed enough power to demolish the spaces they inhabited. These tightly engineered "machines," such

Vito Acconci. *The Peoplemobile*, 1979.
Mobile installation (Amsterdam/Rotterdam/Middleburgh/Eindhoven/Groningen).
Truck, steel panels, vinyl, audio. 24 panels, 2 x 60 x 84 in.

# PERFORMATIVE ARCHITECTURE

### MAKING A SPACE

If the space presented is complete, what's left for the viewer is to relive the space—this is the domain of fiction, the impulse is preservation (conservative); if the space presented is not yet complete, what's left for the viewer is to try out the space, attempt the space—this is the domain of essay, the impulse is change (radical).

### VEHICLE/ARCHITECTURE/PROPAGANDA

The viewer activates (operates) an instrument (what the viewer has at hand) that in turn activates (builds) an architecture (what the viewer is in) that in turn activates (carries) a sign (what the viewer shows off): the viewer becomes the victim of a cultural sign which, however, stays in existence only so long as the viewer works to keep the instrument going.

### FLOOR AND WALL

Granted the impossibility of experiencing and analyzing at one and the same time; granted that a wall to be in front of (analyze) is too much summary ("the writing on the wall"), while a space to be inside of (experience) is too much fantasy ("lost in space")—an artwork can have the best of two worlds, asking a viewer to make, inside, a private space (home) for self while making, outside, a public space (monument) for others. (An artwork, then, should require a group: a work that allows one viewer at a time can be used as a justification for collectors, for private ownership.)

### COLLISION OF SIGNS

Politics, in order to maintain itself as a system, in order to keep its definition, is forced to simplify; while art, as a category of loose definition, might have (when working as politics) the luxury of thickening the plot, having both sides at once, showing the other side of the coin. (It would follow, then, that an artwork goes counter to the existent organization, whatever that organization might be: in a socialist system, e.g., an art-agent might be obliged to do capitalist art.)

—VITO ACCONCI
*Some Grounds for Art as a Political Model*, 1981

as *VD Lives/TV Must Die* (1978) and *The People Machine* (1979), functioned like catapults or oversized slingshots—one snapped cable would set off a Rube Goldbergian chain of destructive events. In these installations Acconci placed viewers in unusually commanding positions, a reminder of the power world leaders—and individual citizens—have at their disposal.

Acconci's last major work of the 1970s, *The Peoplemobile* (1979), is in retrospect a work plan for how his art would develop over the next two decades. A simple flatbed truck fitted with a facelike mask, *The Peoplemobile* was driven into public squares in cities throughout Holland. The truck hauled to each location minimalist steel panels that a crew offloaded and configured into a different arrangement each day. On the first day, the panels were bolted together to form a wall and staircase. On the second, they were reconfigured into a three-part shelter. On the final day, the panels took the form of a table flanked by two benches, the most inviting arrangement. A loudspeaker on the top of the truck was used to address the public—more of Acconci's boisterous propaganda—linking this artistic infiltration to other forms of terrorism.

*The Peoplemobile* was not only a compendium of past Acconci ideas; it also predicted his work of the 1980s and beyond. Like many of Acconci's works of the 1980s, the steel panels in *The Peoplemobile* represented basic minimalist shapes that, through human involvement, could be transformed into symbols of everyday life (furniture, wall dividers, shelters). Acconci replaced the site-specificity of his 1970s installations with a new "portable art" that could travel from place to place. By devising "sculptures on the move," he invented a new hybrid of public art and public address. *The Peoplemobile*'s playful flatbed design (a veritable toy truck for adults), complete with humorous Halloween-like mask, eventually reveals an artwork filled with pointed, even acerbic commentary that addresses significant issues. Perhaps most profound, this work, rife with metaphors and allusions, attacks not only the senses but also the mind. It makes viewers think about themselves, the world they inhabit, and about the nature and role of an artwork.

Over the course of a dozen years, Acconci moved from the creation of works that existed only on the printed page to the notion of using an entire city as a gallery space. In his works of the early 1980s he eventually abandoned his use of "time-based" media, such as video and sound, and began to develop his own unique breed of sculpture.[6] His new works included simple geometric forms often arranged in playful variations that, when combined with playground-like viewer interactions, made basic statements about politics, society, and

Vito Acconci.
*Middle of the World*, 1976.
Wright State University,
Dayton, Ohio.
Wooden construction, rope,
four-channel audiotape.

Vito Acconci.
*The People Machine*, 1979.
Aluminum, cable, fabric, audio.
Approx. 33 x 47 x 49 ft. (variable);
swings: $1/4$ x12 x 36 in.;
catapult: $1/4$ x 12 x 192 in.;
ball: 24 in.; flag: 18 x 54 ft.

# ROOM DIVIDERS

1982
Corrugated aluminum,
spray enamel, door track
16 units, each 96 x 192 x 24 in.

A set of eight walls that can be slid on tracks to form different enclosures inside a space.

The walls are made of corrugated aluminum, eight feet high: four walls are eight feet by sixteen feet, and four walls are eight feet by twelve feet.

In their original position (which may or may not be returned to during the course of the installation), the walls make a rectangular, boxlike enclosure in the middle of the space.

If a person wants to enter the enclosure, the wall facing the person can be slid to one side. Now, however, there's another wall in its place, a wall whose handle becomes accessible only after the first wall has been slid all the way to one side. If the person slides the second wall aside, the enclosure has been broken into—only to form a different enclosure, a U-shaped space that blocks off half the room.

A person might then go to the walls opposite, parallel to the first set of walls. Sliding these walls aside results in two boxlike enclosures on either side of the room.

In order to get into these boxes, then, sliding the walls results in the formation of four boxlike enclosures, one in each corner.

The walls are painted, each alternating corrugation, landscapelike (forest camouflage, autumn leaves, blue and green sea). Parts of the unpainted corrugations, then, are painted to form letters: fragments of loaded words, words like *abortion*, *welfare*, *euthanasia*, and *terrorist*. Just as the walls make physical divisions within the space, they function as markers for psychological and social divisions: they divide the people in the space into sides.

—VITO ACCONCI

human interaction. In essence, viewers became part of simple object lessons about their role in society.

While Acconci wryly tempted viewers into action in his works of the late 1970s, it was not until 1980 that he found an active role for his audience in works he termed "self-erecting architectural units." *Instant House* (1980) continued his exploration of governmental power, a theme he first developed in works such as *The American Gift*.

Vito Acconci.
*Instant House,* 1980.
Flags, wood, springs,
ropes, pulleys.
8 x 21 x 21 ft. (open)

*Instant House* begins as four simple wooden panels joined together at the bottom corners and placed on the floor, leaving a large square open space in the center. The exposed side of each panel is covered with the American flag. Hanging above the center square is a swing that, when sat on by a single viewer, pulls the panels together to form a small house. Cutout sections on the front and side panels resemble, alternately, a door and windows or a simple boxlike face. Quite unexpectedly (and observable only to someone standing outside the work), the underside of each panel is covered by a Soviet flag, now revealed on the exterior of the house. Acconci reduces countries, and their ideologies, to signs. Symbolically, the piece seems to enclose the viewer within the "American house," while leaving communism outside, but the placement of the flags on opposite sides of the same panel also suggests that the artist sees these two political systems as merely two sides of the same coin. Made while Ronald Reagan was running for office on a platform of renewed Cold War ("evil empire") sentiments, *Instant House* now serves as a reminder of the decades-long power struggles between two superpower nations. The transformation that the viewer sets off in *Instant House* can also be considered in psychosexual terms—the rising of the panels is analogous to the male erection.

The link between Cold War politics, potency, and male aggression is even more apparent in *High Rise* (1980), in which a multistory series of *Instant House*–like shapes rise from the floor to reveal an upright penis. The number of stories (and thus the size of the penis) is dependent on the sheer strength (power) of a single participant, who uses a go-cart to erect the building. In *Raising the Dead (and Getting Laid Again)* (1980), a viewer sits on a swing to elevate four female mannequins, each painted red.

When the mannequins reach their upright position, they closely surround the viewer. Revealed on each mannequin's back is a poster of a "potent" male political leader (Lenin, Che Guevara, Malcolm X, and Mao Tse-tung).

In *Collision House* (1981), one of several works from this prolific period that utilize a bicycle as an activation device for a sculpture,[7] a more complex architectural transformation occurs. The piece begins as two opposing geometric wedges made from corrugated aluminum and set on a long track. The effort of the bicyclist, who is placed within the first wedge, pulls the two shapes together. The "nose" of the wedge containing the rider eventually breaks the other wedge into two similar forms. When aligned with the first wedge, the three forms become a continuous architectonic interior space, marked with the phrases "BMB. SHLTR. NO. 1" and "BMB. SHLTR. NO. 2." The central portion pushed forward by the nose now stands alone. Visible only to others in the gallery, this section, now with open sides, has become its own house, complete with pitched roof, gold columns, painted cloud shapes, and sky blue walls.

Text plays a more prominent role in another major work of this time, also made from corrugated aluminum. *Room Divider* (1982) consists of eight corrugated aluminum "walls" that are movable on tracks to create rooms. The walls are painted in colors drawn from nature (blue, green). Unpainted areas form letters of charged words like *abortion* or *terrorist*. If more than one viewer interacts with the piece, the walls can either isolate them in separate rooms or bring them together in a large, open space. In certain configurations a partition may open, only to expose another wall, creating a sense of anxiety or the feeling of being "boxed in."

Other works of this period require a group effort to be fully realized. In its inactive state, *Fan City* (1981) begins as four sandwiched aluminum fin shapes that radiate from a central mast. When a viewer opens each of the sandwiched fins, three tentlike triangular shapes are created. This opening action also raises one half-section of two cutout aluminum human figures that are attached to the mast. When another viewer opens an additional set of fins, one more half-figure rises to the top. In order to raise all of both figures, four people must open *Fan City* to its full position, which now resembles a carousel of equal-sized tent shapes. Viewers can also pull on rings that cover the tents in pennant-like swathes of fabric emblazoned with words that designate the zones they establish: gays, nymphos, blacks, pinkos, junkies, freaks, etc. As in *Room Dividers* and, perhaps, as in real life, Acconci's name-calling rhetoric creates divisions among people.

In works such as *Room Divider* and *Fan City*, the viewer is never certain who is actually doing the name-calling—there is no clear, apparent voice (are the viewers calling each other these names?). While Acconci's presence played a significant role in his works of the 1970s, in these later works the participant takes center stage. He has, in essence, left viewers on their own to discover (and even learn from) these imaginative

# COLLISION HOUSE

1981

Aluminum, wood, fabric, enamel, cable, pulleys

9 x 15 x 45 ft.

***Two conventional abstract geometric structures whose collision results in the making of three conventional "real" structures.***

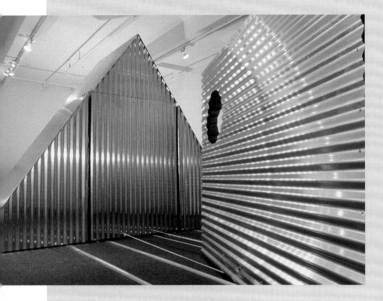

Two wedge shapes, like slices of cheese: the wedge in the middle of the space stands on its end, the wedge at the end of the space sits on its bottom. The wedges are made of corrugated aluminum.

The wedge at the end of the space can be entered from behind: there are two holes cut into the sides, toward the front. The holes serve as windows for a viewer inside. Inside the wedge is a bicycle. A viewer, then, can ride the wedge toward the standing wedge.

As the viewer riding the wedge approaches the standing wedge, the central portion of that wedge breaks off and pulls away from the viewer. The wedge that the viewer is riding becomes wedged between what is left of the standing wedge: two wedges now on either side of the rider. Each wedge has a doorway cut out of its front, the inside of each wedge is painted a cold refrigerator white and a seat is installed on the diagonal rear wall. There's a sign—black letters on white—on the rear wall of each wedge, over the seat: the wedge on the left announces itself as BMB. SHLTR. NO. 1 and the wedge on the right announces itself as BMB. SHLTR. NO. 2.

What had been the central portion of the standing wedge now stands off in the distance, available not to the rider but only to other viewers. The collision has resulted in the making of a pavilion: pitched roof, gold columns, open sides, blue sky, and clouds on the front and back walls. Hanging down between the columns, in the middle of the pavilion, is a black flag with cut out letters: NGGR. FLG. NO. 1. —VITO ACCONCI

new objects. Although the swings, bikes, levers, and other devices lend a user-friendliness to these "architectural games," they can at times put participants in cramped spaces and highly controlled situations, not unlike those of Acconci's installations of the 1970s. In contrast to the wandering spaces of his installations, however, these new sculptures appear more like single, iconic sculptural forms.

Acconci's house works are not entirely sculpture, nor are they architecture per se. Combining aspects of both—along with elements of installation art, furniture, industrial design, and assemblage—these works of the 1980s repeatedly refer to architecture or, more aptly, the *image* of architecture. The rising walls, movable floors, and shifting planes in these works can be best understood as dramatic "acts" of architecture. They are *about* architecture in the sense that architecture can be reduced to an image. Within this context, Acconci's approach is similar to that of architects such as Philip

BMB.
SHLT:
NO. 1.

Johnson or Michael Graves, who in the 1980s freely appropriated elements of furniture (Johnson's Chippendale-style pediment for the AT&T building) or ancient architecture (Graves's myriad classical motifs) for their monumental buildings. Acconci's practice is essentially the inverse; he begins with sculpture and borrows the language of architecture to create what he calls "personal monuments."

Acconci was able to elaborate on these themes when he moved his practice out-of-doors to create "monuments for the public." In 1983 he was commissioned to create a large public work at Artpark, a public sculpture garden in Lewiston, New York. The work, titled *Sub-Urb* (1983), plays on the notion of suburbia through a sequence of inverted houses situated literally below the ground (traditional pitched roofs become the angular floors of the complex). A flat roof at ground level supports Astroturf panels, half of which are movable on a track. A single block letter is "drawn" into the Astroturf, like a manicured lawn. When the panels are pushed together, words are formed (SLUT, BUM, B.O., REB, on one side; SCUM, MUD, B.C., ROB, on the other). When the panels are pushed to the middle, the word SUB-URB is created. The American flag, viewable through the open panels, is painted along the length of each interior

Above:
Vito Acconci.
*House on the Ground,* 1986.
Adobe brick, wood.
3¹⁄₂ x 64 x 26 ft.

Opposite:
Vito Acconci.
*Bad Dream House,* 1984.
Wood, brick-face, shingles,
Plexiglas, screen.
18 x 24 x 25 ft.

side. Access to the work is possible only when a panel is slid over to the middle to expose a staircase. The rooms below, each shaped like an upside-down house, become sanctuaries from the world above, just as suburbs provide refuge from traditional cities.

Acconci played with the shifting angles of inverted houses again in *Bad Dream House* (1984; realized in a different configuration in *Bad Dream House No. 2* in 1988). In this monumental work two inverted brick houses provide the support for a third house made of glass, which rests precariously between the two brick houses. All three are connected to form a confusing, twisting, and almost nightmarish interior space (an antithesis to the idea of "home, sweet home"). The "roofs" of the inverted houses, which now serve as floors, are painted sky blue, while the "floors," which are overhead, are painted grass green. The interior also features upended steps that can be used as seats. The perched glass house, a play on traditional garden rooms, features mirrors, clear panels, and other fun-house devices that break the upper floor into private alcoves for individual viewers.

A slightly different architectural reorientation is evident in a major permanent installation at New Mexico State University in Las Cruces, titled *House on the Ground* (1986). Built into an empty lot using the traditional adobe brick of the area, this large-scale, site-specific structure features four levels of interior spaces that dig their way sixty-four feet into the ground. A façade of exposed brickwork and wooden roof supports, a symbol of New Mexico vernacular architecture, rests at ground level, as if fallen down. It serves as the roof of the structure. The "windows" of the façade provide small entrance portals leading to individual dwellings of alternating size and configuration—zones where individuals can reflect and small groups can interact.

At the same time that Acconci was expanding the proportions of his house works in large-scale public works, he was also developing more intimate sculptures that doubled as furniture. While the large works explore how individuals function within public spaces, his elaborations on furniture investigate a more personal space. In 1985 he articulated some of the reasons why he was interested in developing furniture: "Furniture is midway between clothing and architecture. The way the skin covers the

bones, clothing contains the body: a chair, then, contains the body-contained-by-clothing—a room, then, contains the body-contained-by-clothing-contained-by-chair. Furniture is one move out of privacy, one small step toward going public."[8]

*Ladder Lounge Chair* (1984), one of Acconci's first furniture sculptures, is made from sections of aluminum ladders, functional objects he previously used to build seesaws in a 1979 installation called *Decoy for Birds and People*. Now he bolted together ladder sections to create a seating device that could be used as a lounge chair or reconfigured into an upright "beach" chair. He used ladders in a similar way in *Bridge Chairs (for Sex and Gender)* and *Bridge Chairs (for Argument and Compromise)*, both 1984, in which two ladders meet to provide seating for interaction between the sexes or other groups. Ironically he designed the *Bridge Chairs* so that they could be converted back into traditional ladders, thus providing the participants with a means of escape from their potentially contentious situation.

In 1984–85 Acconci created a number of multipurpose works that function as shelter, furniture, storage, meeting place, or even decoration. *Storage Unit (for Things and People)* (1984) is a combination chest of drawers/lounge chair squeezed into roughly forty cubic feet. When closed, the structure is a sleek paneled monolith covered with Astroturf on one side and velvet on the other. When a viewer pulls on the Astroturf side, the sculpture opens to reveal spacious storage units and a lounge chair. The velvet side opens into a leg rest for the chair and an additional storage bin. *Head Storage* (1985) takes a more playful form—the top section of a human head. This wall cabinet provides a range of storage compartments, some of which are accessible only through mirrored doors or drawers. When put to use, it organizes possessions into discrete compartments, like parcels of information stored in specific regions of the brain. Not only does this work acknowledge our continual need to store our things, but its head shape also points to the "capacity" of our own minds.

Acconci soon began to enlarge his furniture forms so that they could become gathering places for larger groups. These works often forced viewers into specific "positions" in which their bodies "conformed" to the shape of the sculpture. For *People's Wall* (1985), he inserted seating into a thirty-inch-wide room divider. Within the divider are cutouts of adult-sized bodies assuming various positions, including a fetal position, a seated posture with arms upright as if reading a book, and what appear to be sexual positions. In order to become part of the sculpture, viewers must maneuver their bodies into one of the positions. Once a viewer has successfully become part of the sculpture, it soon becomes apparent that this entails a loss of "freedom," specifically freedom of movement. Acconci has, once again, successfully gained a position of power over his audience.

Acconci's largest furniture work of this period is *Maze Table* (1985), a twelve-foot-square sequence of small raised tables and low benches that connect to form mazelike channels. Acconci made the work, initially designed as an experience for the visually impaired, entirely from three-eighth-inch plate glass as a way to "de-emphasize, to as great a degree as possible, the physical presence of the piece."[9] Here, as in many of his furniture works, he was less concerned about *Maze Table*'s apparent function and more interested in the ways visitors would interact with the object. Upon entering the work, the viewer is caught in a game of twisting and turning, almost like a mouse in a cage. When the piece is occupied by a group, viewers find themselves dodging or sitting in front of, or next to, one another. *Maze Table* is another example of how Acconci uses the museum or gallery as a laboratory in which social situations can be created.

Acconci brought his unique language of furniture into the world at large through various public projects using the materials (Astroturf), images (human body), and ideas (the mind, the sexes) from his smaller furniture works. For both *Face of the Earth* (1984; realized again in 1988) and *Sexopath (Parting of the Ways)* (1985), he used the form of the body to create seating in public areas. In the former, seating was created from the orifices of the eyes, nose, and mouth. The latter took the form of a figure bisected up the middle by a path. Viewers had to choose to sit on the female side (designated by the suggestion of a dress) or the male side, or to simply pass through (penetrate) the body.

Conversely, in a series of works made during 1985–87, Acconci brought images and materials of the landscape (the outside world) into gallery spaces and other interior settings. Using a range of found objects (tires, garbage cans), along with plants, dirt, rocks, and other natural materials, he constructed beds, chairs, and bridges for use by one or two people. In works such as *Houses up the Wall* (1985), *People Plant*

Above:
Vito Acconci.
*Face of the Earth,* 1984.
Astroturf, wood.
2 1/2 x 28 x 28 ft.

Opposite:
Vito Acconci.
*Head Storage,* 1985.
Wood, glass mirrors.
78 x 114 x 36 in.

(1986), *Garden Chair* (1986), *Garbage Seating* (1986), *Flower Bed* (1987), and *Hole in the Ground* (1987), viewers could enjoy personal hovels made from disparate yet familiar materials. Acconci extended these ideas in public projects of this time, such as *Palladium Underground* (1986), created as a kind of oasis within the dark basement of New York's Palladium nightclub, and *Garden of Columns* (1987), an employee gathering place located within the Atlanta headquarters of Coca-Cola.

Acconci Studio (Vito Acconci, Luis Vera, Ron Ervolino). *Land of Boats,* St. Aubin Park, Detroit, 1987–91. Concrete, grass. 30 x 170 x 48 ft.

As a result of an increasing number of public commissions during the late 1980s, Acconci was able to explore other unexpected juxtapositions and transformations. In *Land of Boats* (1987–91), made for St. Aubin Park in Detroit, he used a lakeside location to create a playground out of concrete boats that rise unexpectedly from the ground. The overall scheme for the project also takes the shape of a boat, thus bringing to land what is normally found on water. One of Acconci's most perverse public works of this time is *Floor Clock* (1989), a seventy-foot clock built into the floor of a public plaza in Chicago. The numbers on the clock provide seating, but only until the minute hand, which crosses halfway over the numbers, slowly nudges the person off.

The early 1990s were a particularly productive and fertile period for Acconci. Although he was spending an increasing amount of time on public works and architectural projects, he also created several series of remarkable furniture-based sculptures, which he exhibited in traditional gallery settings. Instead of relying on common architectural or furniture forms, these new objects resembled familiar items (clamshell, bra) enlarged to surreal proportions. *Convertible Clam Shelter* (1990), like other furniture works of this period, was designed to be presented, and therefore used, in several different configurations—the two halves of the clam could be opened up, propped at a right angle, or forced together to create a more enclosed shelter. Instead of backrests or steps that force users into common seating positions, the concave shape of the clam allows them to rest, recline, gain shelter, or otherwise conform their bodies to its interior (the exterior is adorned with real clamshells). *Convertible Clam Shelter* is also fitted with its own interior lighting and two audio systems—on the interior, speakers play ocean and other soothing sounds, while the exterior sound system blares conventional noises from the "outside" world (television, radio, etc.)—so that it serves as a self-contained entertainment and relaxation center. The concept of the full-service home entertainment center was carried forward in other works of the 1990s, including *Virtual Intelligence Mask* (1993), a masklike device featuring small televisions, a radio, and two surveillance cameras (which capture in real time what is seen on the TVs), and *Tele-Furni-System* (1997), a jungle-gym-like arrangement of video monitors used as seating for those viewing other monitors.

*Adjustable Wall Bra* (1990–91) is closely related to *Convertible Clam Shelter*. It too is an oversized interpretation of a common object and can be "strapped"

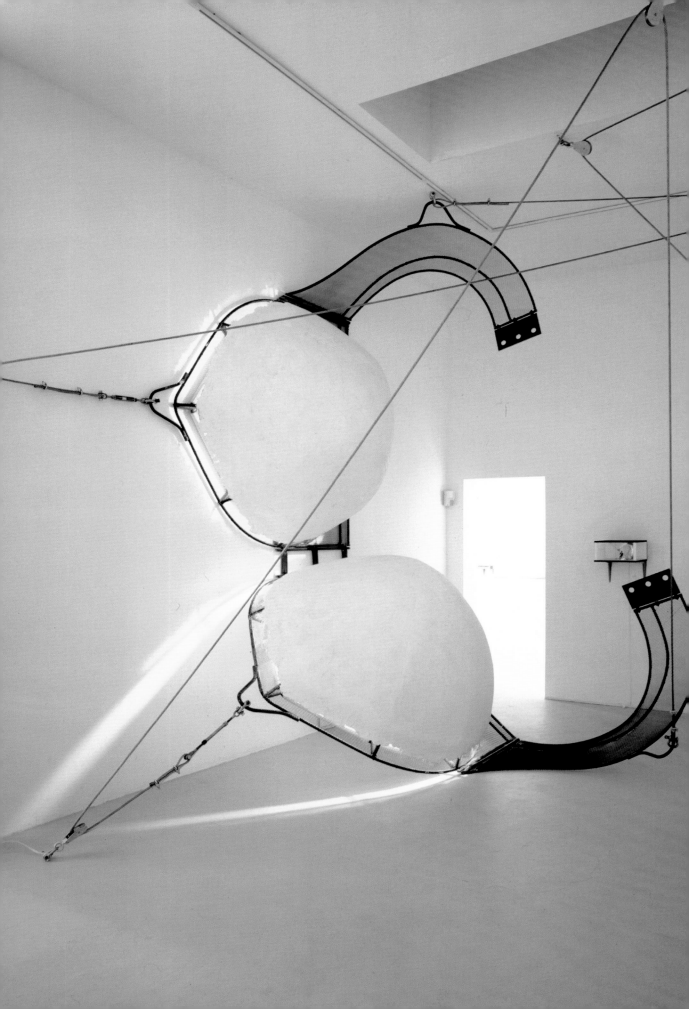

# ADJUSTABLE WALL BRA

1990–91    Steel, lathe, plaster, cable, lights, with audio    Variable dimensions (each cup 96 x 96 x 36 in.)

**An edition of six bras for the wall.**

This is a bra that's worn by a wall; the bra is the height of a conventional wall and is made like a wall, skinned with metal lathe covered with a rough coat of plaster.

The bra is a multifunctional fixture for the home; it functions as lighting, audio speakers, and furniture. From inside each cup, light spills out past the uneven plaster edges and through the metal lathe, onto the wall around it and into the room. The bra has its own sound, steady breathing that pans from cup to cup, into which is mixed input from any conventional sound source—radio, stereo system, television—which is heard then with an undercurrent of heavy breathing. Inside each cup a canvas backing, like the lining of a bra, forms a sling seat.

In its basic frontal position, one cup is stood next to the other, against the wall and facing out, like bulges from the wall. Or one cup might be turned out from the wall, at a forty-five-degree angle—a person might go around and sit, coddled, inside the bra. If both cups are slanted out from the wall, away from each other, a person can sit in each cup, sitting in the same bra but separate from each other, as if in a private capsule. If the bra is pushed into a corner, one cup on one wall is squeezed against the other cup on the adjacent wall. Or the bra might make its own corner, one cup at right angle to a wall while the other cup is at right angle to the first, forming a room. If the bra is reoriented, one cup might be set up against a wall, while the other sits pushed up against it on the floor. Or the wall cup can be tilted out, at a sixty-degree angle, so that a person can squeeze in and sit inside, close to the wall and secluded: another person, in the meantime, might be sitting on the floor cup, as if on a mound of earth; the floor cup, too, might be tilted up at a thirty-degree angle, so that a person can crawl under it and use it as a tent. Or the cup on the wall might be tilted up until it's at a right angle with the other cup, standing on the floor: a person might sit inside the standing cup, facing the wall, under the roof of the wall cup above. If the wall is high enough, one cup might be fixed higher up on the wall so that the lower cup can lean against the wall, at a forty-five-

degree angle, as a lean-to shelter. Or the bra might be lifted up as high as possible, with one cup flat up against the ceiling and pushed up by the other cup against the wall just below it.    —VITO ACCONCI

to the wall in various configurations. It also functions as both furniture and multipurpose center. Acconci's choice of the bra shape is particularly noteworthy. From a psychoanalytic perspective, the work fulfills an infantile longing to return to the mother's bosom (as well as alluding to men's postadolescent fixation with breasts). The amplified breathing sounds that emanate from speakers within the cups of the bras also evoke a yearning for the safety and comfort of mothering.

In the two furniture series that followed, Acconci returned to simpler geometric formats. His five-part Multi-Bed series (1991) features wild combinations of plain gray beds. The headboards and footboards have built-in light panels that add both functionality and visual interest. Each combination creates not only different sculptural arrangements but also unique scenarios for the viewer. In *Multi-Bed #1*, for example, four short beds are mitered together at their "feet" to form a Greek cross. Participants must lie nearly on top of one another in order to fit within the space created. Some of the beds can be reconfigured by the viewer through winches and pulleys. In *Multi-Bed #3*, two beds are joined at their feet. Their shared footboards can be raised to bring the viewers' feet toward the ceiling. Operating another winch reverses the position, allowing the viewers to face each other in a V formation. The most complicated arrangement is found in *Multi-Bed #5*, in which one stationary bed is surrounded by winch-operated beds on three of its sides. Endless combinations exist in what eventually becomes a nightmarish, surrealistic arrangement of sleeping apparatuses.

Acconci's 1992 series of fluorescent furniture works represents an even more reductive vocabulary. With their elegant shapes and striking illumination, these works stand in sharp contrast to the more eccentric machines he created in the 1980s. Using slotted aluminum panels to house ordinary fluorescent light tubes, he made simple illuminated furniture forms—including a bed, chairs, sofas, and tables—that bathe the participant in white light. *Extendable Fluorescent Ladder-Back Chair* (1991) includes a telescoping back that can extend nearly thirty feet in the air to create a towering column of light. Acconci carried these simple, self-illuminating seating forms into a series of cut-sphere benches made for Klapper Hall Plaza at Queens College, New York.

One can trace the minimalist furniture forms seen in these fluorescent works back to the steel panel arrangements that were part of Acconci's *Peoplemobile* of 1979. *The Peoplemobile* also provided the model for a 1991 work called *Mobile Linear City*, a piece of "movable architecture" consisting of five telescoping aluminum units that can be pulled out to create a "city on wheels." When fully extended (in another rather ingenious act of architecture), the work becomes a 130-foot-long partitioned living space. Like its precursor, *Mobile Linear City* can travel from city to city; each unit conveniently fits inside another, so the entire "city" can be compacted and moved to another location. Walls in each unit fold down into a table, chair, bench, and shelf. The last, and therefore smallest, unit functions as a "community service center" and contains toilets, a stove, and a refrigerator. The end wall can even be folded down to make a porch.

Acconci Studio (Vito Acconci, Luis Vera, Jenny Schrider). *Mobile Linear City*, 1991. Truck tractor and flat bed, corrugated galvanized steel, grating, chain, fluorescent light. 13 x 22 x 130 ft.

Other public works of this time demonstrate Acconci's ever-increasing ambition and imagination as well as a further refinement of his well-rehearsed themes. For *Personal Island* (1992), created as a temporary work on the edge of a lake in Zoetermeer, the Netherlands, he found a way to create a private experience for a viewer within an otherwise public space. In its inactive state, the work began as two small rowboats positioned as mirror opposites—one embedded in the ground, the other in the water at the edge of the lake. The landlocked boat, with its oars buried in the ground, appeared to float on a sea of grass. By entering the other boat and activating the oars, a participant could row the boat, along with a circular section of the park, into the lake to create a personal island space. Acconci used a similar strategy in *Park up a Building* and the related *House up a Building*, both from 1996. Instead of bringing the landscape into a body of water, *Park up a Building* brought the *idea* of landscape up the side of a building through a series of telescoping tubes that attached themselves to the roof. The tubes supported small platforms that both held single trees and provided small spaces for viewers to inhabit—the ultimate merging of person, city, and landscape.

During the 1990s Acconci's architectural practice (the Acconci Studio) was vigorously involved in a number of collaborations, interventions, and other projects that were integrated into buildings, streets, and plazas. In 1993 Acconci collaborated with the American architect Steven Holl on a renovation of the façade for the Storefront for Art and Architecture, a small, multipurpose gallery space on the edge of SoHo in New York. The project was born out of an intensive collaborative exercise. As one critic described the process: "The design idea…was born in the *intervening space* between Vito Acconci and Steven Holl. …One of the two men formulated numerous thoughts, and these were either spontaneously discarded by the other or developed further in a discursive process. In a certain sense one man passed his idea on to the other, allowing him to work with it until eventually the first man would be confronted with the result. This creative exchange produced a dynamics which could not be

# MULTI-BEDS

### 1991   Galvanized steel, nylon, foam, Plexiglas, light, cable, winches   54 x 36 x 78 in. each

**Five types of interconnected single beds.**

The headboard and footboard of each bed are galvanized steel frames; the headboard is a mirror outside and a lightboard inside, while the footboard is a mirror inside and a lightbox outside. The foam mattress is covered with heavy gray nylon, the kind conventionally used on suitcases or tumbling mats; the mattress is set on a sheet of expanded metal and riveted to the bed frame.

**MULTI-BED #1.** Two beds crossed so that they are fused together and share a middle. If a person lies on each bed, one person would have to lie on top of or under the other in order to fit.

**MULTI-BED #2.** Two beds crossed so that, in order for each to keep its own full length, one half of each bed is pulled apart from the other half. A person, lying down on either bed, would have to straddle the gap in the middle; the lower part of the person's body would collapse into the hole; a person might use each half of each bed more easily as a seat than a bed.

**MULTI-BED #3.** Two beds placed together end to end, sharing a footboard mirrored on both sides. The beds are joined to each other and the ceiling by cable, with a hanging winch (a come-along) on each side. Operating one winch raises the common footboard, so that the beds slant down away from

each other; two persons, one lying on each bed, would lie with their legs lifted and their torsos brought down, one person would be out of sight of the other. Operating the other winch raises each headboard and fixes the common footboard to the floor, so that the beds slant toward each other; two people, one on each bed, would be lying down as if sitting up, their bodies raised toward each other.

**MULTI-BED #4.** Three beds placed together side by side, headboard next to footboard next to headboard. The beds are joined to each other and to the ceiling by cable, with a hanging winch (a come-along) at the middle of the bed. Operating the winch squeezes the three beds together, accordion-like, one bed slanting down toward the second while the third bed slants away; two people, lying on the beds slanted toward each other, fall into each other automatically, and would have to grab onto the edge of the bed to keep from being together—two people, lying on the beds slanted away from each other, would have to hold onto each other to keep from falling down, into the corner of the beds or onto the floor.

**MULTI-BED #5.** One bed fixed to the floor, with beds on three sides connected to it and to the ceiling by cable. Three winches are set on the headboard of the fixed bed; one winch raises the bed at the headboard—its footboard is lifted, the bed slants down the headboard it shares with the fixed bed; the second winch raises the bed at the footboard—its headboard is lifted, the bed slants up from the footboard it shares with the fixed bed; the third winch raises the bed at the side, its footboard slants past the headboard of the fixed bed while the headboard slants past the footboard. When all three winches are operated, a person lying on the fixed bed is encroached upon by the surrounding beds, and the persons lying in them (one person falls on top from the side, another dives down at the head, another stands like a guardian at the feet).

—VITO ACCONCI

attributed to one individual artist."[10] Acconci and Holl replaced the existing façade with a movable wall in which sections could be opened, folded down to create furniture, or adjusted in other ways to break down the solidity of the building's front. In this way, they allowed light, air, and other elements from the outside to reach the interior space.

Bringing the outside in (and vice versa) has been a repeated challenge for Acconci in his architectural projects. In 1992, for a permanent work at the Arvada

Acconci Studio
(Vito Acconci, David Leven,
Celia Imrey, Luis Vera,
Jenny Schrider, Saija Singer).
*Walkways through the Wall*,
Wisconsin Avenue Concourse,
Midwest Express Convention
Center, Milwaukee, 1998.
Colored concrete, concrete,
steel, light box floor.
14½ x 68 x 204 ft.

Opposite:
Acconci Studio
(Vito Acconci, Luis Vera,
Darío Nuñez, Azarakhsh
Damood, Thomas King).
*World in Your Bones*, 1998.
Details.

Center for the Arts and Humanities, outside Denver, he created an enormous wall of glass and galvanized steel, enclosing different-colored layers of earth, within the center's interior spaces. The work begins outside, where the glass wall emerges from the ground to create a literal "raising of the earth." The wall is paired with a post and lintel structure of a constant twenty-four-foot height, which is shaped like a G clef, announcing one of the functions of the multi-use arts center. The earth wall continues inside the building, increasing in height and attaching itself to the concrete wall, which also continues its path into the interior, through classrooms, offices, and exhibition spaces. Niches and benches were also created within the earth wall to provide seating. For a convention center in Milwaukee, Acconci allowed exterior sidewalks and paths to penetrate the building's façade and gain access to the interior spaces. In certain instances the sidewalks, once inside, "fold" themselves into furniture shapes to provide seating. Conversely, inside walkways continue outside onto a plaza to create benches and a bus shelter.

At present the Acconci Studio is devoted almost exclusively to large-scale architectural projects, although Acconci himself continues to work on conceptual projects and inventive architectural exercises. One such project, *World in Your Bones* (1998), is an elaborate proposal in which a structure ("the world") can actually be screwed into the bones of a participant. This work would become the ultimate amalgam of Acconci's work since 1980; in theory, the structure would provide shelter, seating, an office, a bed, even transportation and a host of other amenities that would "conveniently" be part of the body. *World in Your Bones* brings Acconci's practice full circle. The artwork and the body have become one again, just as he proposed in his groundbreaking performance works of the early 1970s, in which the body became the

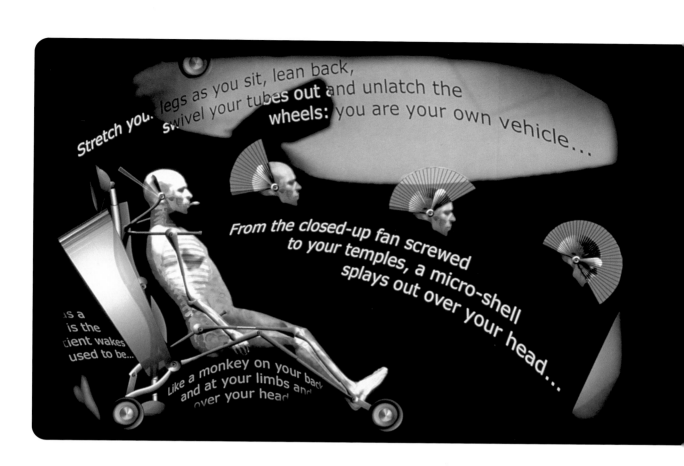

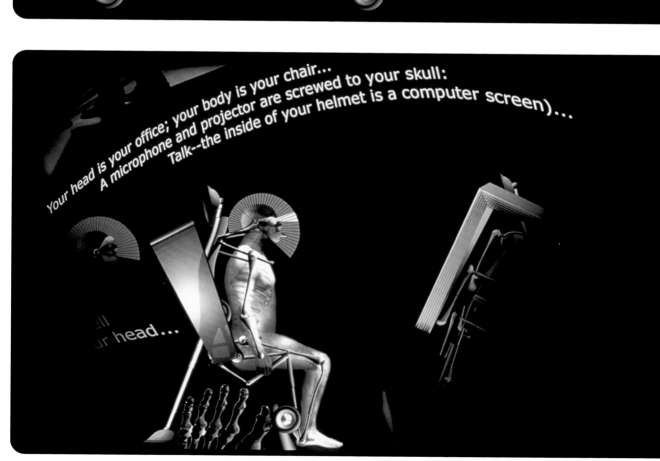

object on display. There is, of course, one important difference in this recent work. Acconci has swapped his body for ours.

Acconci's art has taken many forms over the past forty years, from typewritten pages to entire city plazas. He has developed new categories of art that combine aspects of established art forms (sculpture), more recent traditions (installation art, video), and, most significantly, the practices of architecture, landscape architecture, and furniture and industrial design—fields considered outside the sphere of "fine art." In doing so, he has shattered long-standing functional and stylistic hierarchies.

Certain themes and motifs appear consistently throughout Acconci's career. Beginning with his language pieces and early performance activities, he established a system of examining the "self" through his art. He initially presented his own body and voice to raise ontological questions about his place in the universe. By actively involving the viewer, first in installations in the 1970s and then in architectural games and furniture works in the 1980s, he allowed participants to consider their own being and to interact with others. In his public works of the 1980s and 1990s he brought the art and, with it, the audience out of the gallery and into the world at large to test notions of the self within the broader cultural sphere.

Acconci's art has always been quintessentially urban. His early wandering pieces, in which he walked behind unsuspecting participants, are models of the interactions millions of city dwellers experience every day. In his large-scale public works, he created clusters of small dwellings and microcosms of real-life cities. His *Mobile Linear City* reflects the needs of a modern, completely transient urban culture.

In his art Acconci has often rehearsed various systems and structures found in society, such as group dynamics and gender politics, continually returning to traditional gallery or museum spaces for the exhibition of his work. He used these familiar and easily controllable spaces as stages or platforms to test theories and make allegations about the world around him. While arresting visual qualities were often found in his art (the beautiful cut plate glass in *Maze Table* or the captivating light in the 1992 fluorescent furniture series), his art has never really been about formal issues. He has always been concerned, first and foremost, with content and subject matter. Ultimately he has attempted to make art that makes us think and, ideally, take action.

Acconci's art always seems to reveal something unexpected. With slight modification or physical effort, viewers can transform a sculpture into something entirely different. He continually confounds expectations by bringing the outside in and the inside out. He has turned houses upside down, situated building façades on the ground, brought boats onto land, and allowed the landscape to enter buildings. He has blurred the line between artist and viewer, between the product of the creative imagination and "reality." And in the process, Acconci has helped to reshape our ideas about the artist's role, compelling us to discard our sometimes clichéd or romantic notions in favor of a new concept: the artist as one who refuses to leave things alone.

## NOTES

Designations such as "performance situations," "portable art," "sculptures on the move," "self-erecting architectural units," and "architectural games," which are used throughout the text, are Acconci's own terms for his work.

**1**   Excerpt from a text for the installation *Plot* (1974), originally shown at the Galleria Alessandra Castelli, Milan, December 1974–January 1975.

**2**   Kate Linker, *Vito Acconci* (New York: Rizzoli, 1994), 13.

**3**   Quoted in *Avalanche*, no. 6 (fall 1972): 4.

**4**   Acconci outlined his notion of people as "regions" in David Rosenberg, "Notes from a Conversation Tape with Vito Acconci," *A Space News* (July 1971); later excerpted in Lucy Lippard, *Six Years: The Dematerialization of the Art Object from 1966 to 1972* (New York: Praeger, 1973), 243, and Linker, *Vito Acconci*, 35.

**5**   A page from a transcript for the audio track of *Where We Are Now (Who Are We Anyway?)* is reproduced in Linker, *Vito Acconci*, 91.

**6**   One exception to Acconci's abandonment of "time-based" media is *Mobile Home* (1980), which includes an audio track.

**7**   Other works of this period that utilize bicycles are *Mobile Home* (1980), *Trailer Camp* (1980), *American Pop* (1980), *Sliding Doorway* (1981), *Community House* (1981), and *Exploding House* (1981).

**8**   Quoted in "Homebodies," in *Vito Acconci: The City inside Us* (Vienna: MAM–Österreichisches Museum für angewandte Kunst, 1993), 79.

**9**   Quoted in Andrea Miller-Keller, *Matrix XX: Vito Acconci*, exh. brochure (Hartford, Conn.: Wadsworth Atheneum, 1998), unpaginated.

**10**   Quoted in *Acconci/Holl: Storefront for Art and Architecture* (Ostfildern: Hatje Cantz, 2000), 38.

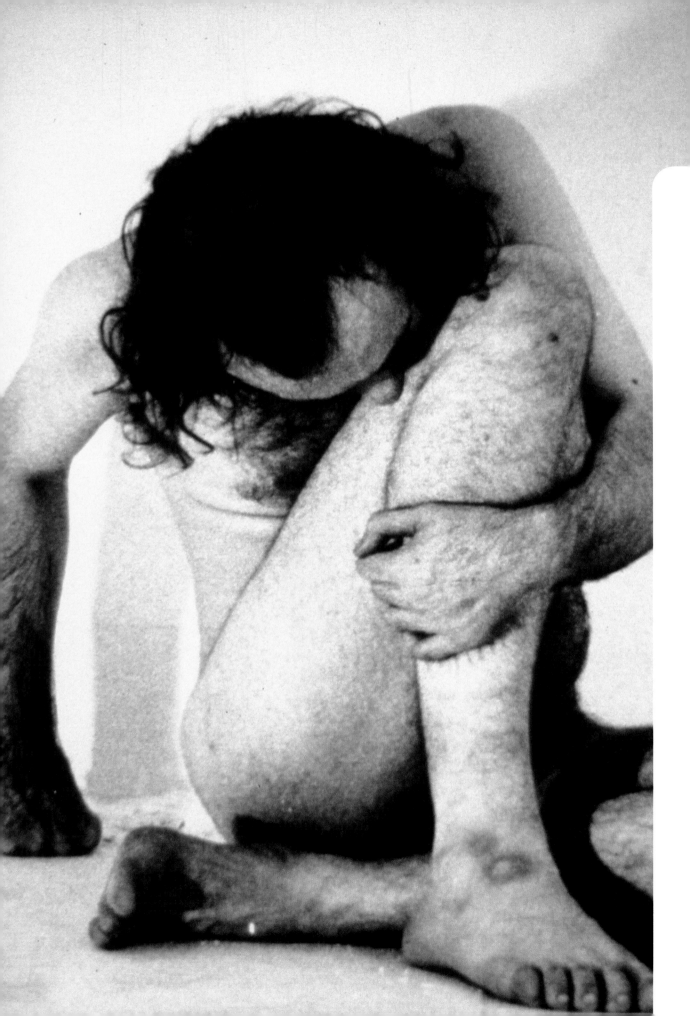

# SAINT ARCHITECT OF SODOM

SANFORD KWINTER

Vito Acconci masturbates in public, grunting and calling out obscenities to us as he goes about it.[1] He locks himself blindfolded in basements, excoriates us for intruding, menaces us with implements of harm, but ensures that we come.[2] Other days he follows us in the street, anywhere we go, and God knows we can't shake him— not ever!—not, at least, until we arrive at a policed boundary that separates the private *us* from the public *him*.[3] Naturally it pisses us off to have to do this, but how else to rid ourselves of this barely civilized nuisance? Acconci, we tell ourselves, like some latter-day Diogenes, is crazy.[4] We've always said that. Everyone does.

So why is everything in Acconci always opening up and either beckoning or forcing us in? Why does he want everything right in his face—or even further still—*in his orifices*?[5] Why is it all hanging out?

What is the body but a pattern of open and closed patches, and patches that are simultaneously, or alternately, both? If so, this holds not only for the physical, biological body but for the social body and the body politic as well. How and when something is opened and closed determines everything about its life. Making a life—among other lives—is no more or less than a performance, a performance of opening and closing these patches, of performing or composing the patchwork of life. Every act of opening and closing is at once a social, political, and sexual act. Each of these acts is a performance not only of opening and closing a patch of space but also of linking the different continuums of bodies (physical, social, and political desire) together within the single and same ecstasy— or misery. What are our personal and collective lives but orchestrations

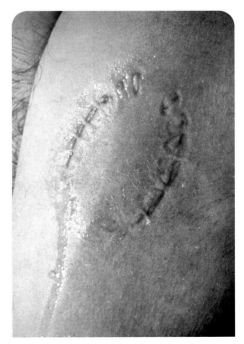

Vito Acconci. *Trademarks,* 1970. Activity (biting).

of ecstasy and misery, patterns of desire modulated and kept dynamic by an unpredictable system of opening and closing, damming and release?

But damming something up by no means promotes only misery, and ecstasy need not be associated only with release. Ecstasy is derived not simply from the opening but also from the broader, more promiscuous *performing*: from the discovery that the relations of life are plastic and that the world is amenable to manipulation. All performance is the performance of freedom, the freedom to recompose the world-patchwork, to eroticize collective life by opening what's closed and closing what's open, while repudiating the myriad and silent political acts of nonconsensual sodomy.

There is a privileged realm from which the concept of performance has been able to take on its broader ecumenical meaning—not sex, not politics, not society alone, but aesthetics. The Marquis de Sade played everything out from within confinement, likewise the great Jean Genet. Each found the incipient plasticity in the closed keep of his jail cell and performed egregious, ecstatic openings with language, imagined deputy selves, even feces and blood. To this litany of materials Vito Acconci has contributed saliva,[6] sweat,[7] come, taped obscenity,[8] and, of course, humor, always humor. More than anyone else he gave a name and an identity to a practice that had not yet separated itself from the messy business of affirming the primordial drives in the face of their social and political annihilation. Before Acconci we could think of literary manifestations, of speech acts and their perturbing effects on the material world, only as the products of a "voice," but after him we see the world as a system of performances that we do and undo and that are done and undone despite us. In Acconcian performance, art, desire, and activism are one.

Acconci began his career with nothing at all, nothing but a place and his body and its drives and the specificity of those drives being *in that place*. The place was the city, the body was not his own, but rather was his body cast as the first-and-not-yet-formed-body, as an any-body-whatever, "per"-forming—creating—itself in relation to the existing overtrained, oversubdued bodies of the modern world. When Acconci found himself in the streets of New York in 1969 and began to follow random citizens one by one until he could pursue them no further (because prevented by the consensual boundaries that define private space),[9] he was no different from the adult foundling Kaspar Hauser, who appeared mysteriously on the streets of a small German town one day in the nineteenth century, and to whom all culture, including language, was entirely foreign. Yet bit by bit, though never completely, Hauser became "naturalized," and his story concerns not so much "the enigma"—from where he came—but, on the contrary, how he became civilized, how he endured the mortifications and impositions of culture.[10] Likewise, Acconci's early work (from the years conventionally understood as the "performance period" [1969–72], when he produced almost all the works alluded to above), enacts not only an ontogenesis (genesis of the human individual) but a cosmogenesis as well.[11] For world and self, Acconci has tirelessly shown us, are generated together. This means that the one can always be dismantled through the other as well.

Did reperforming the world in this way make Acconci crazy, or was the craziness presupposed in the first act of placing himself outside the world (as a not-yet-formed-body), ready to be fucked by it for our collective amusement and edification? Acconci does not perform just his own (self) formation but the formation of the world

# FAN CITY

1981   Aluminum, fabric, cable, pulleys   12 x 24 x 25 ft.

***A group of wedges that fan out into a city of tents.***

Four aluminum fin-shaped structures, twelve feet long and six and a half feet tall at the highest point, extend, in a cross shape, from a central mast. Each fin structure is composed of a sandwich of two fins, inside of which are what appear to be vertical aluminum bars, the height of the fin shape, packed together and each holding a roll of colored fabric. At the mast, two cutout aluminum figures—streamlined human shapes—bisect each other and the central pole; the bottoms of the figures are enclosed in a black steel box that holds the mast and onto which the figures are hinged.

Each aluminum sandwich has one static fin and one movable fin; the base of each movable fin extends out from the other and can be used as a handle. A viewer can grab hold of the handle and push or pull the fin so that it moves clockwise; if the fin is pulled out as far as it can go—up to the next static fin—it pulls out with it three tent frames (the vertical bars have extended out into shape, making a tent composed of two vertical bars in front, two horizontal bars at the floor, and a diagonal bar down the middle, going back to the central mast). As each fin is pulled out, one half of one of the aluminum figures rises up the mast: the bottom of the figure resembles a fish or a bomb. If all four legs are pulled out by viewers, a whole circle of tents is erected, and the aluminum figures are joined together again at the top of the mast.

While a viewer keeps holding the handle, keeping the fin out and the tent frames extended, another viewer can pull a ring at the front of any of the tents, drawing out fabric from a shade roller at each of the vertical bars, and making side walls for the tent. The fabric is in the shape of a college-football pennant; each pennant is about six feet by twelve feet, covering the side of the tent. If all the fins are pulled out, so that all the tent frames are extended, and if all twelve rings are pulled on by viewers, all the tents have sides, all the tents are, in effect, "named." The pennants have words (in American Egyptian typeface, like college-football pennants); the words label the dwelling places for inhabitants of this city: one quarter reads, in shades of blue, GAYS, PUNKS, NYMPHOS—one quarter reads, in shades of green, BEGGARS, CRIPPLES, OLD FOLKS—one quarter reads, in shades of brown, BLACKS, ALIENS, PINKOS—one quarter reads, in shades of red, JUNKIES, SCHIZOS, FREAKS.

When the viewers let go of the rings, the pennants retract; when the viewers let go of the fin handles, the tents fold up and the fins return to their starting point.

—VITO ACCONCI

## LADDER LOUNGE CHAIR
1984    Aluminum ladders
144 x 42 x 36 in.

An eleven-foot ladder, in five irregularly sized sections, hinged together: the ladder can be folded out to form a lounge chair or a beach chair.

—VITO ACCONCI

as well as its necessary correlate. In his initial, still parochial art worldview, the world was represented by the gallery, an appallingly clean, white anus definitively sealed off from any public sphere. No wonder Acconci went deliriously "dirty."[12] Like many in those years, he felt compelled to move outside and away from the political and cultural infrastructure of the gallery, yet he remained oriented toward it. In the gallery he discovered the codes and diagrams of a more silent and insidious performance of power, an enforced system of enacted openings and closings. Acconci (alongside Robert Smithson and Daniel Buren) discovered *the wall* as the ambiguous foundation of culture, body, and consciousness.[13] His cosmos thus came increasingly to embrace architecture as its final destination and limit case. Architecture is that in relation to which bodies are organized, made, and unmade free. Acconci made architecture crazy in a way that no architect has ever been able to. One might say that he seeks to achieve for architecture what Sade and Genet did for literature— to transform the world-prisonhouse into the privileged place from which to conceive and to invent freedom.

The body in Acconci represents both the origin and the end of all things. Architecture, by contrast, represents the ecstasy of the body but also the body's pain. The body is also the architecture of the private self, however, simultaneously the domicile and the performance of the self. Did not Freud teach us this? A body is born, but the self is *that which emerges* as the drives organize on its once promiscuous and polymorphous and—yes, why not say it?—perverse surface. The self emerges like a vortex on an agitated sea increasingly punctuated by blockages, disaggregations, sectoring, and the cumulative pocking that is the inescapable residue of experience. The surface breaks up into organs, or more accurately, we should say that the body's organs become the convenient anchors and way stations of the colonizing self. The body's "features" become "organs" only once the self has settled into them, appropriated them into their own landscape of perspective and need. The born body is nothing but mouth: receptive, open, continuous, and fluid.[14] World and self have not yet emerged.

Yet the threshold is near. Subsequent development concerns the necessary passage through the anus and no longer the mouth, or rather through that recessed place at the depths of the mouth whose very discovery represents the discovery of unfathomable depth itself and the internal darkness that accompanies it. The oral surface gives way to internal depth, a place not accessible to the light of the world. Self splits away from everything else, and everything else becomes world. As Gilles Deleuze and Félix Guattari once wrote: "The first organ to suffer privatization, removal from the social field, was the anus. It was the anus that offered itself as a model for privatization."[15] The person or self is formed in the anal stage, Freud tells us, when both the products and functions of this body part must be removed from the social sphere. The dark, interior place is the realm of the private self and its formation, the foundation of private life. But the anal stage must be surpassed in order to arrive at the final or genital sphere. If the anal stage is the scaffold for the formation of the private person, the genital stage is that of the public one. To accede to genital existence, it has been long argued, is primarily to accede to the regime and the domain of the phallus/penis. (Female genitality, as the cliché goes, is an acceding to "lack" and "envy," which is a priori an acceding to the phallus.) The double character of genitality allows the penis to remain quasi-private and hidden from view, while the phallus is left free to circulate openly and publicly, to distribute relationships, hierarchies, structures, mores, customs, desires, and the relations among their agents. In a phrase, it literally engenders the social world.

A body's history, quite simply, defines what a body is. Our history is the history of both our personal and our collective bodies, the history of how and when and why and where we permitted this or that patch of our existence to be opened or closed. Our social world, like our personal one, is cleaved in one particular manner rather than another because it is designed to function in the service of calculated ends of which we generally know little. For Acconci the organization and cleaving of the world in *this* manner—a decadently rich private world, on one side, and an impoverished public one, on the other, with none but the most rigid and routinized connection between them— are both arbitrary and unacceptable.

Against the cleaving of the world, and against the arbitrary imposition of boundaries and walls, Acconci proposes a performance and practice of the *hinge*. In Acconci the hinge takes a great many forms. Rarely a banal and fixed hinge, it is much more often a promiscuous and articulated fold, a magically flexible erotic device that grows and contracts and slips and slides, assembling and disassembling in a perpetual act of play and tumescence, involution, connection, and humor. The hinge may be a literal hinge, as in *Instant House* (1980), or a rotational vulval matrix of flaps and fins, as in *Fan City* (1981), or else it might be an algebraic-geometric hinge like the phallic, continuous inside-outside passage found in *Klein Bottle Playground* (2000). In every case the continuity between inside and outside, public and private, is enacted, or performed, like a tender public act of fornication.

These spaces are never inert or complete in themselves. Not only do they always constitute social spaces and both demand and imply the existence of human agents, but they are activated, completed, *turned on*, only with human energy and effort. The *Ladder Lounge Chair* (1984), for example, displays a range of "modes": it is sometimes vertically erect, and then, at other times, it recedes back into poised horizontal folds to receive a body into itself. Similarly, the magnificent *Adjustable Wall Bra* (1990–91), one of Acconci's most famous works, hinges and sprawls all over a room like the rolling heat of sex itself seeking the exquisite maximal state between frenzy and control. It is hard and soft at the same time, not quite tectonic but decidedly erectile and savagely sexy, because not only does it open to draw us in, it welcomes us to relax and to become breasts ourselves. After *Convertible Clam Shelter* (1990), who could ever gaze upon a clam in quite the same way again or see it as anything but a flexible amalgam of tits, pussy, womb, and ass? Of course almost everything opens to reveal an interior and to reveal or complete a desire, to make the heat of bodies transit from here to there. The hinge doesn't just connect; it provokes a total modulation of openness and closedness. It throws up an infinitely adjustable universe of polymorphous social connection in which desire does not retreat into privacy, doubt, or shame[16] but projects

# CONVERTIBLE CLAM SHELTER

1990   Fiberglass, galvanized steel, clamshells, rope, lights, audio
Variable dimensions (approx. 96 x 120 x 36 in. each half)

*An edition of five clams, each the size of a small room and each adjustable into five kinds of habitable spaces.*

Each shell is about ten feet by eight feet, two feet deep. The shell is made of fiberglass, the inside surface smooth and pearllike, while the outside is coated with hundreds of clamshells, like bricks or stones, adhered with resin.

The clam is hinged and can be locked into its various positions; embedded into the half shells are cleats, with nautical rope attached—when the clam is opened into a particular shape, that position is stabilized by tying the necessary ropes to cleats on the ground.

**POSITION 1.** The clam lies on its back, the upper shell lifted open about eighteen inches: the clam functions as an enclosed bed, a kind of hiding place to squeeze into.

**POSITION 2.** The clam is stood on the edge of its short side, its hinge at the back and the shells open to a width of about three feet: the clam functions as an alcove, a set of walls making a dead end.

**POSITION 3.** The clam is stood on the edges of its long side, its hinge at the top and the opening enlarged to six feet: the clam functions as an arch.

**POSITION 4.** The clam lies on its back again, the upper shell raised at a forty-five-degree angle to a height of nine feet: the clam functions as housing, like a lean-to tent.

**POSITION 5.** The clam is pulled open, one shell lying next to the other, the space between the far edges about thirteen and a half feet: the clam makes its own ground, its own landscape—a place to sit in, sprawl over, lie down in.

The clam provides its own light. Inside the clam, under the "ledge" of each shell, light shines through a Plexiglas crescent cut into the fiberglass.

The clam provides, also, its own sound. Each shell encloses a speaker. There are two sound sources, one from inside the clam and one from outside: panning from shell to shell is the sound of water, waves, ocean—mixed into that, above and below it and behind and in front of it, changing sounds are drawn from any conventional sound source (radio, stereo system, television) in the room.

—VITO ACCONCI

outward into endless invention…and laughter.

In *Multi-Beds* (1991) a coiling winch collapses an accordion of adjacent beds to press the coupled bodies into one another (pairs coupled in the cave of the *V*) or else to demand the improvisation of new positions for those who must maintain contact while being wedged around the vertex of two outward-tilting planes. "Open" or "closed" in itself matters not at all here, for the ecstasy, as always, lies in the discovery and performance of plasticity, in the invention of new copulas.

The traditionally overprivatized, overly precious anality of the architectural profession could not but be fascinated by Acconci's expulsive audacity. *Park up a Building* and *House up a Building*, both from 1996, are brilliant and (to use an expression employed by the Ben Kingsley character in the recent film *Sexy Beast*) notable for their sheer *fuckoffness*. They flout their host structure with unapologetic parasitism and in-your-face trespass while thumbing their noses at the repressed programmatic interiority of the museum. They literally perform something akin to the spoken obscenity of "opening it up and sticking it in." An exquisite, but not obvious, precursor

Vito Acconci/Steven Holl. *Wall Machine,* Storefront for Art and Architecture, New York, 1993. Supraboard, plaster, steel, hinges. 9 x 100 x 14 ft.

## PARK UP A BUILDING
1996   Aluminum, grating, trees and tree bags, fluorescent lights   Variable height x 36 x 7 ft.

**PROGRAM.** A portable park adaptable to a blank wall of any building.

**ORIGINAL SITE.** Alvaro Siza's museum building, Centro Gallego de Arte Contemporáneo, Santiago de Compostela, Spain.

**PROJECT.** Nine pairs of telescoping tubes, U-shaped at one end and L-shaped at the other. The U-shaped ends hook onto the parapet of the building; from the L-shaped ends, one module of a park is suspended on threaded rod.

Two types of park-module alternate: a floor with a seat on opposite sides, inside and outside, and a floor with a seat on the inside and a tree on the outside. A connector, a step, joins one module to another.

The floor, the seat, and the step are metal grating— you can look up through them; the tree is enclosed within a metal grate, its roots encased in the burlap sack it was transported in. A light from beneath each floor illuminates the park. Each successive module is hung one step higher than the one before: as you walk through the park—as you walk from step to floor, between seat and seat and between seat and tree— you're climbing up the side of a building.

The tubes, the park hangers, telescope down to eight-foot sections, so that they can be transported and adjusted to buildings of different heights. The park can be hung with its companion unit, HOUSE UP A BUILDING, on different walls, or the park can be hung alone.

—VITO ACCONCI

to this work is *Wall Machine* at the Storefront for Art and Architecture (1993) in New York City, a project conceived and designed with architect Steven Holl. In this work the front façade of the sliver-shaped gallery is stripped off entirely and opened up to the dirt and drama of street and square. The outer skin is then replaced by a boogie-woogie striptease of pivoting partitions that swivel and wink and jive like a cool jigsaw orgy. This is the gallery par excellence, as Acconci would have needed to imagine it: porous, projective, polymorphous, and intensely *public*.

Acconci's project is only apparently and inadvertently to free our bodies from routinized sex. He knows well that, in contemporary social space, if you're not actually fucking, you're probably getting fucked. For Acconci, the public realm (raised everywhere and assiduously to a concept and an ideal) is the place of exotic, unforeseeable, and utterly egalitarian encounter. And yet today "the public" is defined as no better than a mere residue, the pitifully wanting remains of a land grab waged in the name of privacy. Private space today creates compulsive, private people, private and truncated acts, and private and shameful desires. It is commonly said of Acconci that he is a public artist, a producer of public art. But that is not quite accurate. The public realm, Acconci has proclaimed, is not actually a place, but a mode.[17]

Acconci Studio
(Vito Acconci, Luis Vera,
Won Chang, Robert Bedner).
*More Balls for Klapper Hall*,
Queens College, 1993–95.
Fiberglass, granite finish, light.
13 x 80 x 160 ft.

If Acconci's work appears to have evolved from an abstract, real-time, one-off conceptual format embodied in literally enacted experience (and its recording) to concrete sculptural, architectural, and landscape projects, this is only an illusion of scale. He still is as he has always been, at once a political artist *and* a guerrilla of the carnivalesque.[18] In the carnival one's private places are either displayed or ritually destroyed in order that one be born again, differently.[19] In Acconci, the invention of the performance (the mode) is also the performance of invention itself, the extension into everyday life of the carnival mask and the orgiastic dance. By turning us into ambulatory breasts, for example, he makes us aware of our valency (social *and* erotic) and encourages our capacity to invent new relationships with home (the open, discarded bra). We are freed, one might say, in the same delirious way that Charles A. Reich, in *The Greening of America* (1970), once described the ankles of 1960s flower children as having been liberated by bell-bottom pants (!?!). Contrary to the famous bra burnings of the 1960s, liberation in Acconci is conceived not as the annihilation of constraint, but only *the destruction of its private nature*. His revolutionary project is to destroy not things, but only the artificial and uptight boundaries between them.

This is why every one of Acconci's performance-works is sited in the interface between inside and outside. The development and elaboration of this "boundary" through extension and transgression is exactly what Acconci is denoting by his frequently used phrase "to thicken the plot."[20] All of space and time are the results of scenarios or "plots" that can be reconfigured through dramatic manipulation, by the insertion of individual performance-*plots* that initiate new relationships and new becomings: "A private life makes a deposit into public space."[21] The typical Acconci project consists of an attack on existing space that always begins with an espousal of that space followed by a reversal and an opening of the closed pathways through the private that lead to it. The craziness of Acconci lies in his capacity to continually "out" himself before our eyes, to shamelessly flaunt the shameful. It is not so much a critique as a detonation of social space, a setting it *wild* with jokes, mischief, obscenity, and dance. Acconci knows that social space is constituted by desire, but a desire that has been muffled, corrupted, made predictable by its relegation to the private sphere.

Our built and choreographed environment reflects this corruption, timidity, and doubt. Acconci rescripts the world as a new saintly Sodom to which all of the happy and primordial valence between social actors has been restored. Miscegenation is always the answer, division always the enemy. This is why Acconci can identify pop music as the new model for public art; it is environmental, inclusive, and volatile, providing an outlet for emergent local novelties, idioms, and vernaculars. It forms novel groups, even in the absence of real aggregation. It also provokes corporeal response. But the technical apparatus of our society—our infrastructure—does not fail to engender countermovements, regressions, reprivatizations against which we must maintain our vigilance. Among Acconci's many hilarious performances is the final (twentieth) section of a long text he published in a leading American journal of humanities and letters, a paragraph that consists of only four words.[22] The essay (a methodical working through of the history and theory of public space) signs off with a short section all its own, in which is inscribed the following perverse provocation-rejoinder:

Beware of the Walkman.

And we know he is right. Who brings a Walkman to an orgy?

## NOTES

**1**  *Seedbed*, performance at Sonnabend Gallery, New York, January 1972.

**2**  *Claim*, performance with video installation at *Avalanche Magazine* office, 93 Grand Street, New York, 1971.

**3**  *Following Piece*, performance, New York City, 3–25 October 1969.

**4**  The ancient Greek philosopher Diogenes was known for his public nakedness and onanism, and was commonly said to be mad.

**5**  *Openings*, performance documented on Super-8 film, August 1970, and *Trademarks*, performance documented in photographs, September 1970.

**6**  *Waterways*, performance documented on video, 1971.

**7**  *Runoff*, performance documented in photographs, 1970.

**8**  *VD Lives/TV Must Die*, installation, The Kitchen Center for Video and Music, New York, February 1978.

**9**  "Each day I pick out, at random, a person walking in the street. I follow a different person everyday; I keep following until that person enters a private place (home, office, etc.) where I can't get in" (artist's description of *Following Piece*).

**10**  See Werner Herzog's film *Every Man for Himself and God against All / The Enigma of Kaspar Hauser* (1974), based on this true story.

**11**  In his seminal 1978 text "Steps into Performance (and Out)," Acconci recapitulates the aesthetic universe in pure Cartesian fashion from the foundational and primordial "I" and its capacity to act and enact both the intersubjective and the object-world (in *Performance by Artists*, ed. A. A. Bronson and Peggy Gale [Toronto: Art Metropole, 1979], 26–40).

**12**  Germano Celant, "Dirty Acconci," *Artforum* 19 (November 1980): 76–83.

**13**  Vito Acconci, "Normal Art: Art in Public Places," course at the San Francisco Art Institute, summer 1983.

**14**  In *Trademarks* (see note 5 above), a naked Acconci bit every part of his body that his mouth could reach to leave deep bite marks that could later be ink-printed. This work performed not only a delirious and ecstatic act of autophagy (mouth incorporates and includes everything) but also generalized and extended the primordial oral opening across the entire surface of his body. This was a kind of architectural regression meant to restore every patch that had been closed to its original oral and open state.

**15**  Gilles Deleuze and Félix Guattari, *Anti-Oedipus: Capitalism and Schizophrenia*, trans. Robert Hurley, Mark Seem, and Helen R. Lane (New York: Viking Press, 1977), 143.

**16**  Doubt and shame compose one side of the Ericksonian anal dyad, which places autonomy (of the self) on the other.

**17**  "The words *public space* are deceptive; . . . I'm forced to have an image of a physical place I can point to and be in. I should be thinking only of a condition" ("Public Space in a Private Time," *Critical Inquiry* 16 [summer 1990]: 901).

**18**  Recall the hilarious expulsive scenes of birth and defecation in Rabelais's *Gargantua*. Rabelais served as the foundation of Mikhail Bakhtin's study of carnival; see *Rabelais and His World*, trans. Hélène Iswolsky (Bloomington: Indiana University Press, 1984).

**19**  "You leave your home computer not for the mind but for the body, not for the head but for the genitals" ("Public Space in a Private Time," 910).

**20**  See Vito Acconci, "Some Grounds for Art as a Political Model," in *Art of Conscience: The Last Decade* (Dayton: Fine Arts Gallery, Wright State University, 1980), 6.

**21**  "Steps into Performance," 36.

**22**  "Public Space in a Private Time," 918.

Acconci Studio (Vito Acconci, Ron Ervolino). *Floor Clock*, 1989. Concrete, steel, clock mechanism. 4 x 70 x 70 ft.

# Buildings and Plazas

Public space is an old habit. The words *public space* are deceptive; when I hear the words, when I say the words, I'm forced to have an image of a physical place I can point to and be in. I should be thinking only of a condition; but, instead, I imagine an architectural type, and I think of a piazza, or a town square, or a city commons. Public space, I assume, without thinking about it, is a place where the public gathers. The public gathers in two kinds of spaces. The first is a space that is public, a place where the public gathers because it has a right to the place; the second is a space that is *made* public, a place where the public gathers precisely because it doesn't have the right—a place made public by force.

In the space that is public, the public whose space this is has agreed to be a public; "these are people "in the form of the city," they are public when they act "in the name of the city." They "own" the city only in quotes. The establishment of certain space in the city as "public" is a reminder, a warning, that the rest of the city isn't public. New York doesn't belong to us, and neither does Paris, and neither does Des Moines. Setting up a public space means setting aside a public space. Public space is a place in the middle of the city, but isolated from the city. Public space is the piazza, an open space separated from the closure of alleys and dead ends; public space is the piazza, a space in the light, away from the plots and conspiracies in dark smoky rooms.

The space that is *made* public began as its own opposite. This was a space that was never meant to be public at all: a royal space, or a presidential space, or a corporate space. This private and privileged space had inherent in it, from its beginning, the seeds of public space: the fact of its existence provoked desire, its privacy functioned as a taunt to the public that felt left out. Once that space has been taken over by force and made public, it has inherent in it, in turn, the seeds of private place, the seeds of a redefined and reinhabited privacy: the public that takes it over is working its way up to the royalty or the presidency or the corporate office. Private space becomes public when the public wants it; public space becomes private when the public that has it won't give it up.

—VITO ACCONCI
*Public Space in a Private Time,* 1990

## PROJECT FOR MOSCONE CONVENTION CENTERS 1 & 2

San Francisco, 1991
Glass, mirrored stainless steel,
clock mechanisms, lights
48 x 240 x 450 ft.

The site is a busy street between two convention centers; the program is to connect the buildings so that they exist as one convention center complex.

On each side of the street, the glass or granite walls are used as supports for twelve clock faces; the diameter of each clock face is determined by the size of the wall. The clock numbers are light boxes.

There is every possible time, from one o'clock to twelve o'clock. Each time, each clock, is pulled apart; the hour hand, minute hand, second hand—each is enclosed in its own glass disk, the edge mirrored so that it disappears. From the numbers on the building wall, each clock is stretched across the street: the hour on the sidewalk, in front of the numbers—the minute hand across the street, on a traffic island—the second hand on the sidewalk on the other side of the street. The clock faces from one convention center, progressing from hour hand to minute hand to second hand, are intersected by the clock faces from the other convention center, progressing in the opposite direction.

To tell time, you read through the clock—from one hand to the other, through clock faces from the opposite direction, across people and traffic, to the numbers on the wall. As you walk along the street, or drive down the street, you pass literally through time. As a traveler to the convention center, from another time zone, you have to find your own time, in the middle of all possible times; you have to make your own time.

—VITO ACCONCI

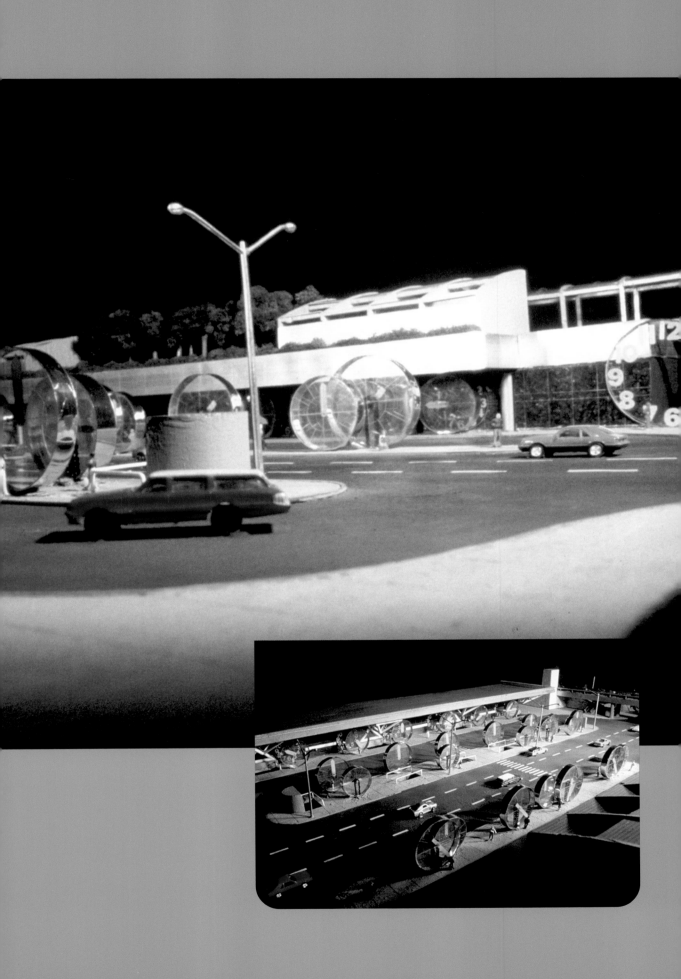

# PRELIMINARY PROJECT FOR LAAKHAVEN/HOLLANDS SPOOR

The Hague, Netherlands, 1993
Water, soil and grass, trees, paving stones, concrete, steel grating
20 x 720 x 780 ft.

**SITE.** A waterfront development: a U-shaped water channel runs through a complex of buildings and plazas and parks (a university campus, offices and stores, private residences).

**PROGRAM.** Activated public spaces that help define the development as a new city center.

**PROJECT.** The earth moved under our feet. The water alongside the land is intertwined within the land: the land drifts out into the water, while water slips in through the land.

Half a landmass is cut away and pivoted out into the water; each successive half of land is halved again and pivoted out in turn into the water. Or a piece of land is pulled out, into the water, letting water flow in to fill the land: another piece of land, then, from the side, is pulled out into the new body of water, letting water flow in further to fill more land. (Where continuous passage is needed, the gaps between pieces of land are covered with grating.)

As the land shifts out, it shifts up or down: a landmass pivots down and sinks under water, while a waterfall flows down over the retaining wall; a landmass pivots up and rises above water, like a glacier, like a ship in a stormy sea.

—VITO ACCONCI

# CIRCLES IN THE SQUARE

Project for Marienhof, Munich, 1998 (theoretical project)
Steel tubing, light, grating, fabric, mirror, glass, polycarbonate, mesh, concrete, asphalt, trees, water
295 x 394 x 492 ft.

**SITE.** An "accidental" plaza that exists as a consequence of bombings during the Second World War; the surrounding buildings here, instead of functioning as the walls of an outdoor room, just happen to be there on the edge. Below the plaza is a subway station.

**PROGRAM.** Make a structure for activities in the plaza, and give reasons for people to be there.

**PROJECT.** The pavement of the square is a large circle filled with smaller circles. Where the smaller circles meet the edge of the large circle, the leftover space is covered with grating and lit from below. You enter the square, you enter the circle within the square, by walking over a void of light.

A complex of spheres sits on the circles: the spheres are open tubular structures, in three sizes, bunched together and interlocked. One sphere intersects another; a sphere above is cradled by spheres below; the lowest spheres settle underground and bulge up above the ground.

In the center of the complex, and interspersed throughout, are Garden Spheres. Around each tree-filled sphere is a ramp, made of grating; the edge of the ramp folds into a bench—you sit within foliage. From the spiraling walkways around the Garden Spheres, you access other spheres, other globes, other worlds. The Garden Spheres are free spaces that lead to programmed spaces.

Two Subway Spheres (through an open U cut out of a blue triangular section, you take an escalator, in between trees and soil, down into the subway station below the plaza); a Parking Sphere; a Market Sphere; a Theater Sphere; an Aviary Sphere (you walk around birds, below birds, above birds); a Skate Sphere (the skateboarders appear as ghosts behind translucent fiberglass skating ramps, like slices out of an orange); a Pool Sphere (the pyramid of the swimming pool extends down into the subway station below; in the station, there's an aquarium of human beings overhead).

Where two spheres interlock, the shared space is closed up with frosted glass. These shared spaces are Service Spheroids (different floors function as toilets, snack bars, storage, maintenance closets, backstage areas, and dressing rooms).

This new plaza, dense with spheres, is a city within the city. The spheres rise like bubbles amid the surrounding buildings.

—VITO ACCONCI

# LANDSCAPE FOR WASHINGTON STATE STADIUM

Seattle, 1999
Concrete pavers, steel structure, water, light, bamboo trees, glass pavers, mesh
27 x 552 x 740 ft.

### Landscape as stadium

**SITE.** A professional football stadium and the exhibition hall behind it.

**PROGRAM.** Landscaping for the stadium and its surroundings. Allowance should be made for a gate system into the stadium.

**PROJECT.** The ground in front of the stadium, and around the stadium, is turned into a stadium.

Strips of pavement are raised off the ground to form bleachers. As the pavement leaves the ground, it's replaced below by water.

The bleachers function as a ground for landscape: trees, from ground level, climb up the bleachers as if rising over a hill; channels of water meander along the bleachers, zigzagging from one row to the next as if down a rocky hillside, and turning into waterfalls as they drop through to the pond below.

The bleachers function as a light source: the ponds, made from the displacement of pavement, are lit from below; light shines up through the bleachers; it reflects off the bottom of the seats and glows onto the surrounding pavement.

The bleachers function as gates: segments of bleachers, at the bottom, are pivoted up to let people through, into a game.

The bleachers function as seats facing different directions; there are platforms between one flight of stairs, one set of seats, and the next—the platforms make areas, walking-and-stopping-places, elevated above the ground.

The bleachers function as miniature stadiums, pocket stadiums that fit into spaces left over by the stadium proper. As the bleachers curve around the front of the stadium, they branch off, inside the curve and outside, to form squares of bleachers; the pavement that remains, in the center of the water, is shifted off to the side and replaced by an island of colored light. You walk across the shifted pavement, over the water, and onto a glowing island. The island might function sometimes as a casual place like a beach in the middle of water and waterfalls; the island might function, at another time, more formally, as a little stage, a pocket theater.

—VITO ACCONCI

# MAK DESIGN SHOP

MAK Österreichisches Museum für angewandte Kunst, Vienna, 2001

### *A Store of Rotating Rings: Products on the Move*

The store is organized by rings. From each doorway, a line of rings makes a corridor through the store. At the side of each corridor, additional rings tilt toward the corridor and intertwine with the rings of the corridor; each of these tilted rings makes the boundaries of a room off to the side of the corridor.

The rings rotate. Each successive ring rotates in an opposite direction: one ring rotates clockwise, the next counter-clockwise, etc. Each ring is a container for inaccessible products, products meant not to be touched. The ring is a circular transparent box, a circular tube (this should be relatively light, so it might be made of polycarbonate); the products are attached to the inside wall of the tube—the inaccessible products circle around you as you walk, they fly over your head and disappear beneath your feet.

Within each corridor, the space between rotating rings is spanned by a curved shelving unit. These shelves might be made of perforated metal. They hold accessible products, products meant to be touched. A shelving unit might start at the floor and come up to the height of your waist; or a shelving unit might start at your knees and come up to your chest. The products here curve up your body as you walk; they're products to grab for, products meant to be touched. There might be light behind the perforated metal, lighting the products from behind.

The floor within the corridor is also perforated metal. From each doorway, the floor within the corridor rises as it heads toward the middle of the store; the rise of the floor allows each rotating ring to pass under the floor—the rise of the floor also allows light to come from below, providing ambient light as you walk.

To the side of the corridor, the elliptical rooms formed by the tilted rings have floors of their own, made also of perforated metal. The floor might fold up at the edge to make shelves; these shelves fill the space between the floor and the tilted ring, thereby making a railing as a by-product. These rooms function, for example, as a room for accessible furniture, which can be sat in—a room for catalogues (you might sit and read in the room), a room for watching video.

The outside wall of the store cuts the ellipse of one of the rooms; the tilted ring that makes the boundary of the room isn't stopped by the wall; the ring continues its rotation outside the building. The counter and cashier's desk for the store are a glass plate fixed over a nearly horizontal rotating ring. As you pay for the products you've bought, more products, inaccessible products, skim past you. The rotating ring of the counter continues out the window, inviting people in the street to come into the store.

—VITO ACCONCI

# PROJECT FOR CORNER PLAZA, CENTER FOR THE PERFORMING ARTS

Memphis, 2001
Two-way mirror, steel, light
42 x 72 x 70 ft.

A swathe of something—it could almost be a liquid—swoops out from under the glass room that juts out over the entrance to the building. This swathe doesn't cling to the underside of the glass box; it barely touches it: it's as if a liquid has been flung up against it and frozen in the air.

The swathe is a flow, a curve, an undulation that sweeps across the plaza and around the corner; the flow peters out: it begins at the height of the glass box and descends toward the ground as it flows—the liquid rolls like waves as it flows. The flow is embodied, the liquid is solidified, into a gob, a glob, a blob that functions as a roof—a far-flung roof—over the plaza. The roof is not an object within the site but an instrument that transfers the site and transmits the site. It's as if the surroundings are formed, and transformed, into a roof. Ideally the roof is two-way mirror (glass or acrylic); from below, where the roof functions as shade, the surface is transparent, you can see through it to the surroundings—from above, where the roof is open to sunlight, the surface is mirrored; it brings down the sky—both above and below, depending on the passage of light, reflection mixes with transparency, and vice versa. The roof might also be opaque mirror, above and below: the sky falls down to the roof, while the ground rises up to it.

Openings are cut out of the roof, and from the rim of each opening the roof is stretched down to the ground like a funnel; each funnel functions as a column that supports the roof. As the skin of the roof is pulled down, an arch is left open below, so that each column can be entered. In the middle of the site, the largest column—eighteen feet in diameter—might be used as a performance area, outside the official theater inside. The middle-sized column—twelve feet in diameter—might be used as a meeting room. The smallest column—nine feet in diameter—might be used for more intimate get-togethers.

At the bottom of each column, the circular wall is shaped into a ring of seats, both outside and inside. Outside the column, if the surface is two-way mirror, you're sitting under a roof, but you're open to the sky; if the surface is opaque mirror, it's as if you're inside; the pavement below is reflected up onto the roof above you—it's as if you're sitting inside the ground. Inside the column, you're outside; the sky is your roof, and sunlight pours down on you from above; the wall that circles around you reflects the sky—you're sitting inside the sky. At night, light comes from the opposite direction; the circle of ground formed by the funnel is a floor of light: light shines up the circular wall of the column, into the sky.

As the roof is pulled down, it's also pulled up. From the slopes of the roof as it waves over the site, from the slopes of the roof as it warps down to make rooms, funnels are stretched up toward the sky. Sunlight comes in and shoots down across the plaza. At night, light goes up; a ring of artificial lights around the hole in the roof shoots light up through the funnel and into the sky; light bounces from side to side across the circular wall of the funnel and shoots back down into the plaza. Where the roof floats into the underside of the glass room, a funnel of artificial light is pulled down to light the entrance to the theater.

—VITO ACCONCI

Acconci Studio (Vito Acconci, Luis Vera, Darío Nuñez, Celia Imrey, Sergio Prego, Rafael Varela, Thomas King, Serena Heres). *City in the River*, Warrington, England, 1998. Steel, aluminum, grating, cable, mirror, lights, fabric, hinges, pontoons, sliding mechanisms, pipes, pumps, water. 120 x 240 x 855 ft.

# Parks and Gardens

"Land ho!": the sailor's cry of discovery, from high up on the mast, as the ship approaches its goal after a life at sea. This is the beginning of the word *landscape*. In order for discovery to be possible, land has to be considered first as far away; land has to be far off so that it can be seen all at once, as a panorama. Land recedes and becomes "landscape." "Landscape" equals "landescape"; the land escapes, out of your reach: the word *landscape* pulls the land away, or pushes you back away from the land—that land now, unused and unusable by you, is free to expand out in front of you. Once the land is in front of you, it isn't land anymore, it isn't ground: the land becomes landscape, the ground becomes a wall, the wall becomes a picture. The word *landscape* is subsumed into the phrase "landscape painting": "landscape" is not just a view of land, it's a picture of land, a picture that comes with its own history and its own conventions of pictorial representation. As a picture, "landscape" is not only seen but also made, constructed, produced. "Landscape," then, comes with an aura of untoucha-bility; it has double safeguards: first, in order to be viewed, it has to be kept at a distance—second, since it is produced and therefore owned and exchangeable, it has to be protected.

Landscape is an attempt to keep land in place, to keep land in one piece, lest it be fragmented and blown to bits by "land mines"—(def.) cavities in the earth that contain explosive charges, just below ground surface, and that are designed to go off from the weight of persons passing over them. On a "landscape," you're in the world of science fiction: passing over the earth in a spaceship, you have a vantage point from which to explore the earth, map the earth. On a "land mine," you're in the world of detective fiction, film noir: you don't have the luxury of looking around you and looking ahead, you have to keep looking at exactly where you are.

A view of the landscape can be replaced by a view to the landscape, and through the landscape. The landscape, instead of being an object for the eyes, becomes an object for the body; instead of being an object of sight, it's an object of touch—an object of the body's insertion into the landscape. Instead of being the passive receiver of sight, the landscape becomes the active agent of motion: the landscape moves as it's subjected to motion, as it's moved into and moved through. The landscape rises and falls; it can be considered as a series of horizontal planes, parallel horizontal planes going from below ground to above ground. These parallel horizontal planes are the infrastructure of behavior; they cut through the body as the body cuts through them. The body drifts through parallel planes of landscape, while parallel planes of landscape are driven through the body.

—VITO ACCONCI
*Bodies of Land*, 1992

# ROUNDABOUT RISE & FALL

Project for Eastern Roundabout, A-13, London Borough of Barking and Dagenham, 1998
Galvanized steel, mesh, motors, plantings, water, light
Variable height x 85 x 85 ft.

A roundabout directs and organizes traffic; it keeps traffic moving. Here it's the traffic that moves the roundabout, that keeps the roundabout going. The roundabout is "made" by traffic; the roundabout changes its shape as cars drive by.

When the roads are empty, the roundabout is only a plot of land, a flat circle of greenery raised no higher than curb height in the middle of radiating roads. But when traffic approaches, the roundabout grows.

The circle of the roundabout is divided into five circles, one inside another, one attached to the other. The outermost circle is fixed, while the four inner circles are movable: each responds to incoming cars from one of the four roads that head toward the roundabout. When a car passes over a sensor embedded in the road, it sets off a motor that activates the one circle of land directly in front of it.

As you drive toward the roundabout, the roundabout comes to life: the roundabout breathes, the ground opens, a disk of land pivots up in front of you. As the ground splits open, water falls; from under the disk, a waterfall pours down into a pool in the middle of the roundabout; light shines up from under the pool; the waterfall glows. You're driving into the mouth of the roundabout; you veer off to the side and circle the roundabout.

Each additional car, crossing the sensor, props the ground further open, to a height of five meters; each additional car after that, then, keeps the ground open, and the waterfall flowing, a few seconds more. As cars approach from more than one road, the roundabout grows: circle upon circle of land pivots open, one on top of the other. The roundabout rises, higher than the elevated highway beside it.

As cars drive away from the roundabout, the land closes, circle by circle; the waterfalls are closed up inside the ground; the roundabout sleeps, ready to wake, ready to tremble, at the first sign of another approaching car.

—VITO ACCONCI

# LAND OF WATER

Project for Heilgarten 2000, Vlotho, Germany, 1998
Water, grass, glass, mirror, steel
40 x 1,536 x 2,724 ft.

**SITE.** In a region of underground mineral waters, a highway connecting Düsseldorf and Hannover.

**PROGRAM.** A bridge over the highway; in the land on either side, a travelers' garden, a respite for car drivers on their way from one city to another.

**PROJECT.** It's as if the water from underground has seeped up to the surface. The water announces itself; the veins of the ground show; the land is veined with water.

Five "rivers" flow down the site in different directions. As a river flows, it tapers; as a river flows, it branches off into rivulets that fan out over the site. The rivers and rivulets flow in concrete V-channels that carve into the ground. The concrete of the channel folds up onto the ground and makes a pathway next to the water; the pathway shifts from one edge of the river to the other. One river connects, through its rivulets, to another; you walk through the site by following the water.

Some rivers, when they reach the slope at the side of the highway, are cut short; they drop off as waterfalls at the side of the road. Other rivers, when they reach a slope, continue out above the road and cross over to the other side. The V-channeled concrete trough that holds the water, within the ground, turns into a channel of glass: a glass bridge that carries the river across the road. As you walk over the bridge, water pours down the sloped glass railing on either side of you, water pours toward you; you walk on glass, you walk on water under glass.

Or you drive under water as you drive under a bridge. You park your car off the side of the road. Where a river meets a road, the asphalt stretches from the road to the river, making a parking lot.

Where a rivulet branches off from a river, a patch of grass in between pivots down, into the ground. You walk into a pocket park; from above, the rivers spill down in waterfalls, over the sides of the park. As the pathway ramps down, an extension of concrete onto the grass remains horizontal and forms a seat. In some of the pocket parks, as the land pivots down, a triangle of land within it pivots up, making the roof of a service area. The walls are two-way mirrors; at night the service area glows. There are toilets here and a canteen; you can get information here. Outside the service area, you might have a picnic on the grass roof.

—VITO ACCONCI

# GARBAGE CITY

Project for Hiriya Garbage Dump, Tel Aviv, 1999 (theoretical project)
Concrete, steel, glass, light, water, grass, crops, gas-processing equipment, solar panels, water plants
394 x 2,362 x 4,199 ft.

**SITE.** A garbage dump alongside the highway to Tel Aviv. In use since 1951, the dump has formed into a mountain, 260 feet high, populated by birds; because the Tel Aviv airport is nearby, there is fear that the birds will cause airplane accidents. The dump is surrounded on three sides by water channels, polluted by the garbage. The view from the top of the garbage dump is the "best in Israel," toward Tel Aviv and the Mediterranean.

**PROGRAM.** Reuse of the dump, keeping in mind that the ground of a garbage dump is unstable and cannot bear foundations for structures.

**PROJECT.** A city formed from garbage, with garbage, and for people.

The slopes of the dump are stabilized by concrete "mesh," an open-grid retaining wall that doubles as a building, or as a ground for buildings

To the south, the concrete mesh is folded out from the mountain and pulled toward the highway. From one side of the dump, the foldout spirals in on itself, forming the bowl of a stadium. From the other side, the foldout spirals around the stadium and forms the shell of a convention center, or a town hall; an office building is plugged into the foldout. Between the foldouts, the trees of a public park break through the wall on cutouts of mesh that pivot down and cantilever over the water channel. This end of the mountain is the public sector of the city; from other cities and towns, people come here for public spaces, and they come here for work.

To the west is the private sector. Here the concrete mesh that stretches up above the slope and tilts outward is a wall for plug-in private houses and a plug-in school, lit from within and illuminating the neighborhood outside; the houses step out from bottom to top, reaching out toward the view.

The city is powered from the garbage it's settled in. At the front of the mountain, a cut of concrete mesh spirals inward to form a power plant; methane gases are drawn out of the dump, and processed gas is distributed to the city. The water channels that flow on three sides are joined together in front and turned into wetlands. On the southern slopes, solar panels are inserted into the grid of concrete mesh. The irregular top of the mountain is leveled into planes, a grazing field for cows and fields for crops; the city sustains itself.

You enter the city from the highway; a road descends underground into a tunnel that comes up onto islands of parking in the middle of the wetlands. From the islands, a monorail ascends the top edge of the rising concrete mesh wall, around the city. You get off the monorail and take a funicular down the wall to your destination.

—VITO ACCONCI

## ISLAND ON THE MUR

Graz, Austria, 2001
Steel, glass, polycarbonate, water, light
18 x 82 x 246 ft.

A passageway across the river morphs into an island in the middle of the river; from above, on the riverbank, a tube descends into the water and bulges into a dome that twists into a bowl that's sucked into a tube that ascends to the opposite riverbank, and vice versa.

The tubes are suspended in air; the dome and the bowl float on the river. The dome and the bowl and the tubes are transparent; they're sheathed in glass, within a steel grid. Water pours down the shell of the dome, into the river; as the surface of the dome twists like liquid into the surface of the bowl, water clings to the outside of the bowl, like water overflowing out of a cup, or out of a bathtub; as the surface of the dome and bowl twist to sheathe the tubes, water flows down from the tubes like waterfalls.

The bowl functions as a theater; the inside of the bowl is lined with bleachers—transparent bleachers, made of grating or perforated metal—that step down to a stage at the bottom of the bowl. When the bowl is not being used as a theater, it functions as a public space, a plaza, in the middle of the river; each line of bleachers waves in and out, it expands and contracts— the bleachers swell out to make little plazas.

The dome functions as a café/restaurant. Just as bleachers descend the edge of the bowl, a ramp spirals up inside the dome. The ramp rises above toilets at the edge, and above a bar counter around a kitchen in the middle; the waving ramp bulges out to make table-and-chair areas closer and closer to the water-covered dome.

Where dome and bowl intersect, and where the dome is transformed into a bowl and vice versa, a playground is formed by the collision and by the melting. This in-between space is a three-dimensional grid, like a space frame; the grid functions as monkey bars, a field to climb up and crawl through and hang onto; slides are cut through the grid. The playground stretches into the dome, at the edges, where there's no headroom for standing adults. The playground is usable both inside, behind the surface of the dome, and outside, on top of the water running down to the inside of the bowl. Functions are mixed on this island; the playground functions in the theater as a backdrop for the stage and in the café as part of the ceiling—one function fluidly becomes another.

Light streams up from beneath the bleachers, in the bowl, and down from the roof structure, in the dome.

—VITO ACCONCI

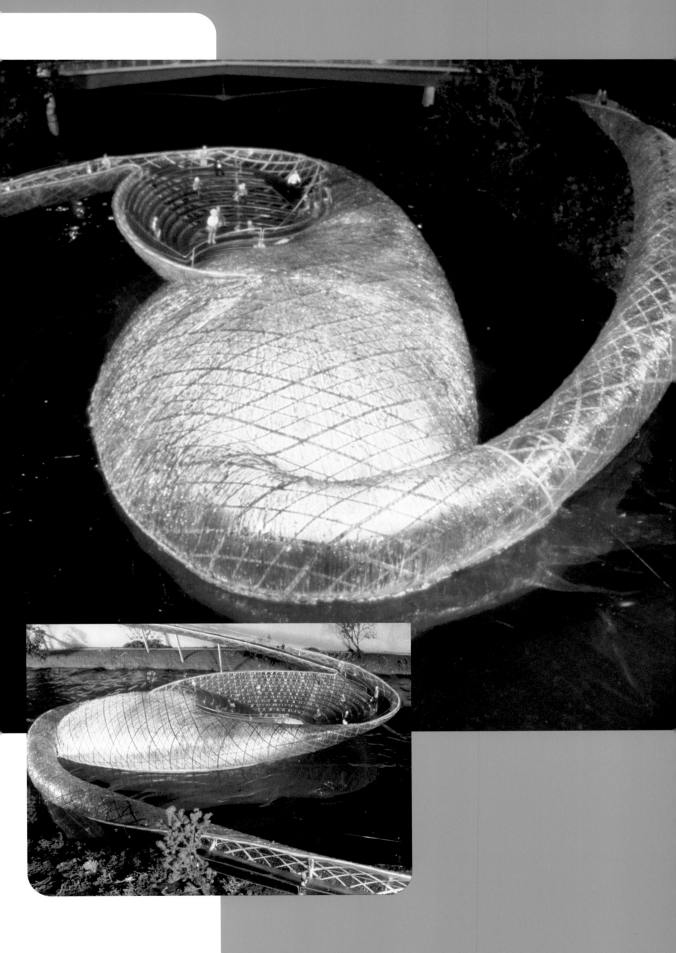

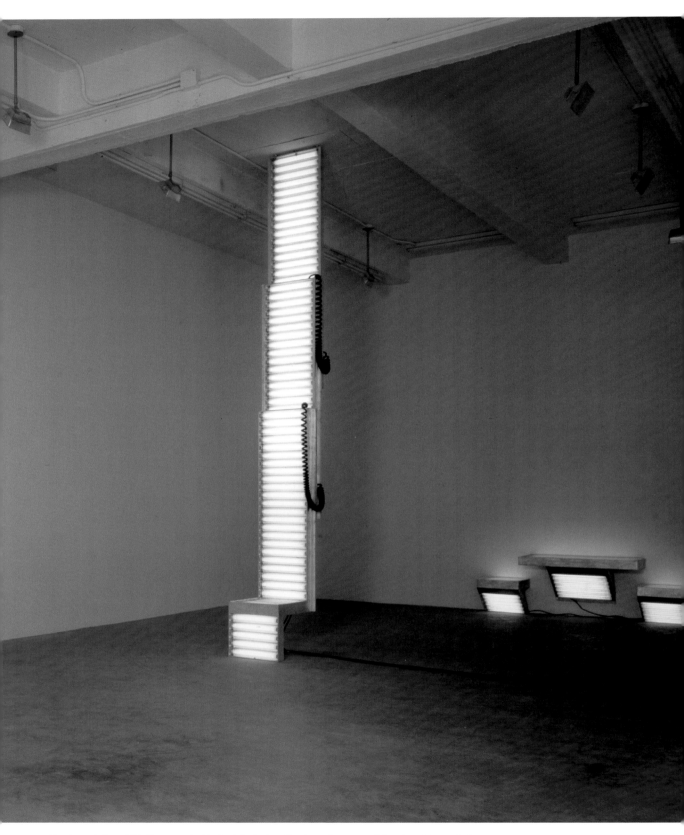

Vito Acconci. *Extendable Fluorescent Ladder-Back Chair,* 1991. Aluminum, fluorescent light tubes. 84 x 24 x 24 in.
Vito Acconci. *Fluorescent Table and Chairs,* 1992. Aluminum, fluorescent light tubes. Table: 22 x 52 x 27 in. Chairs: 17 x 19 x 22 in. each.

# Checklist of the Exhibition

Note:  Height precedes width precedes depth in all measurements.  The works included in the exhibition vary from venue to venue.  Unless otherwise indicated, all works lent by the artist/Acconci Studio, New York.

**Instant House**, 1980
Flags, wood, springs, ropes, pulleys
96 x 252 x 252 in. (open)
96 x 60 x 60 in. (closed)
Museum of Contemporary Art, San Diego

**Room Dividers**, 1982
Corrugated aluminum, spray enamel, door track
Each unit 96 x 192 x 24 in.

**Ladder Lounge Chair**, 1984
Aluminum ladders
144 x 42 x 36 in.
Lent by Michael Krichman, San Diego

**Ladder Lounge Chair**, 1984
Aluminum ladders
144 x 42 x 36 in.
Irena Hochman Fine Art Ltd., New York

**Head Storage**, 1985
Wood, glass, mirrors
78 x 114 x 36 in.
Lent by Lois Plehn, New York

**Maze Table**, 1985
Glass
30 x 144 x 144 in.
Collection of Camille O. Hoffmann,
Naperville, Illinois

**People's Wall**, 1985
Wood, fabric, mirror
96 x 192 x 30 in.
The Speed Art Museum, Louisville, Kentucky

**Hole in the Ground**, 1987
Concrete, rubber, steel, stones, dirt, plates
36 x 96 x 72 in.

**Convertible Clam Shelter**, 1990
Fiberglass, galvanized steel, clamshells, rope,
lights, audio
Variable dimensions (approx. 96 x 120 x 36 in. each half)
Collection of Camille O. Hoffmann,
Naperville, Illinois

**Adjustable Wall Bra**, 1990–91
Steel, lathe, plaster, cable, lights, with audio
Variable (each cup 96 x 96 x 36 in.)
Courtesy Barbara Gladstone Gallery, New York

**Extendable Fluorescent Ladder-Back Chair**, 1991
Aluminum, fluorescent light tubes
84 x 24 x 24 in.
Courtesy Barbara Gladstone Gallery, New York

**Multi-Bed No. 4**, 1991
Galvanized steel, nylon, Plexiglas, fluorescent light,
cable, mirror, winches
59 x 113 x 89 in.
Fonds national d'Art contemporain,
Ministère de la Culture, Dépôt au Musée de Grenoble

**Fluorescent Table and Chairs**, 1992
Aluminum, fluorescent light tubes
Table:  22 x 52 x 27 in.
Chairs:  17 x 19 x 22 in. each
Courtesy Barbara Gladstone Gallery, New York

**Shirt of Pockets/Jacket of Pockets**, 1993
Plastic, zippers, snaps
36 x 36 in. x variable depth

**Virtual Intelligence Mask**, 1993
Wire fencing mask, televisions, radio,
video cameras, rubber, vinyl, aluminum, motor
11 x 21 x 16 in.
Courtesy Barbara Gladstone Gallery, New York

**Ready-to-Wear Music Box**, 1994
Plastic, grommets, snaps, music box movements
18 x 30 in. x variable depth
Courtesy Carl Solway Gallery, Cincinnati

**Tele-Furni-System**, 1997
Multichannel video installation with monitors,
speakers, steel and pipe armature
Dimensions variable (approx. 192 x 240 x 276 in.)
Solomon R. Guggenheim Museum, New York
Purchased with funds contributed by the International
Director's Council and Executive Committee Members: Eli
Broad, Elaine Terner Cooper, Ronnie Heyman, J. Tomilson Hill,
Dakis Joannou, Barbara Lane, Robert Mnuchin, Peter Norton,
Thomas Walther, Ginny Williams

**Model Display System**, 2001
Spandex, wire, chain link, 4 slide projectors, various project
models, mounted photographs, text banners
Dimensions variable

# Biography and Exhibition History

For a complete exhibition history, bibliography, and listing of videotapes, films, and audiotapes made before 1980, please see Kate Linker, *Vito Acconci* (New York: Rizzoli, 1994). Exhibitions accompanied by a catalogue are indicated by an asterisk (*).

Born January 24, 1940, Bronx, New York
B.A., 1962, College of the Holy Cross, Worcester, Massachusetts
M.F.A., 1964, University of Iowa, Iowa City

## One-Person Exhibitions (since 1980)

### 1980

Art Gallery, Center for the Arts, Muhlenberg College, Allentown, Pennsylvania

Atlanta Art Workers Coalition

*Vito Acconci: A Retrospective, 1969–1980*, Museum of Contemporary Art, Chicago*

The Kitchen Center for Video and Music, New York

### 1981

Kölnischer Kunstverein, Cologne; Kunsthaus, Zurich

Max Protetch Gallery, New York

Padiglione d'Arte Contemporanea, Milan

Kitchen Center for Video and Music, New York

University of California, Los Angeles

Young Hoffman Gallery, Chicago

### 1982

*Vito Acconci: Recent Work*, Institute of Contemporary Art at the Virginia Museum of Fine Arts, Richmond

Portland Center for the Visual Arts, Oregon

San Diego State University

University Gallery, University of Massachusetts, Amherst

### 1983

Miami-Dade Community College, Miami

Whitney Museum of American Art, New York

Williams College Museum of Art, Williamstown, Massachusetts

### 1984

Gallery Nature Morte, New York

University of Nebraska Art Gallery, Omaha

Zone Center for the Arts, Springfield, Massachusetts

### 1985

Ackland Art Museum, University of North Carolina, Chapel Hill

Carpenter + Hochman Gallery, New York

City Hall Park, New York

Wadsworth Atheneum, Hartford

Rhona Hoffman Gallery, Chicago

Brooklyn Museum

### 1986

*Vito Acconci: The House and Furnishings as Social Metaphor*, USF Art Galleries, University of South Florida, Tampa; Knight Gallery, Spirit Square Art Center, Charlotte, North Carolina*

Kent State University School of Art Gallery, Kent, Ohio

Palladium, New York

### 1987

*Vito Acconci: Domestic Trappings*, La Jolla Museum of Contemporary Art, La Jolla, California; Neuberger Museum of Art, State University of New York, Purchase; Aspen Art Museum, Aspen, Colorado; Laumeier Sculpture Park and Gallery, Saint Louis*

International Center of Photography, New York

International with Monument, New York

### 1988

*Vito Acconci: Photographic Works, 1969–1970*, Rhona Hoffman Gallery, Chicago, and Brooke Alexander, New York*

*Vito Acconci: Public Places*, Museum of Modern Art, New York*

Galleria Il Ponte, Rome

*Vito Acconci: Installations, Working Drawings, and Models*,
B. R. Kornblatt Gallery, Washington, D.C.

*Face of the Earth*, Hillwood Art Gallery, C. W. Post College,
Long Island University, Greenvale, New York

*Vito Acconci: Photoworks, vidéos, et films super 8, 1962–1972*,
Sous-Sol, Geneva*

### 1989

Barbara Gladstone Gallery, New York

Mai 36 Galerie, Lucerne, Switzerland

Sonnabend Gallery, New York

*Vito Acconci: Models for Public Projects Plus*, Gray Art Gallery,
Jenkins Fine Art Center, East Carolina University, Greenville,
North Carolina

### 1990

James Corcoran Gallery, Los Angeles

*Vito Acconci: Graphic Retrospective*, Landfall Press, New York

### 1991

Barbara Gladstone Gallery, New York

Galerie Anne de Villepoix, Paris

Centre d'Art Contemporain, Grenoble, France;
Museo d'arte contemporanea, Prato, Italy*

### 1993

*Vito Acconci: The City inside Us*, MAK-Österreichisches
Museum für angewandte Kunst, Vienna*

Barbara Gladstone Gallery, New York

303 Gallery, New York

*Vito Acconci: Making Public*, Stroom Haags Centrum voor
Beeldende Kunst, The Hague*

Monika Spruth Gallery, Cologne

Galerie Anne de Villepoix, Paris

Museo de Luigi Pecci, Prato, Italy

### 1994

*Vito Acconci: Name-Calling Chairs*,
Contemporary Arts Center, Cincinnati

*Vito Acconci: House of Streets, Parks, and Plazas*, L'Usine,
Le Consortium, Dijon, France

Williams College Museum of Art, Williamstown,
Massachusetts

*Vito Acconci: A Print Retrospective*, University of Missouri,
Kansas City

Le Musée d'Art Moderne de Saint-Etienne,
Saint-Etienne, France

*Vito Acconci: Private Houses*, American Fine Arts, New York

### 1995

*Theater Project for a Rock Band*, Dia Center for the Arts,
New York

La Crie Centre d'Art Contemporain, Rennes, France

### 1996

*Vito Acconci: Living Off the Museum*, Centro Gallego de Arte
Contemporáneo, Santiago de Compostela, Spain

*Public Spaces*, Klosterfelde Gallery, Berlin

*Vito Acconci: Video*, Monika Spruth Gallery, Cologne

### 1997

*Vito Acconci: Old, Refined, and Re-Viewed*, Stroom Haags
Centrum voor Beeldende Kunst, The Hague

Ota Fine Arts, Tokyo

*Park in the Water*, Laakhaven, Netherlands

### 1998

Barbara Gladstone Gallery, New York

### 1999

*Vito Acconci: Public Art*, University of the Arts, Philadelphia

### 2000

*Vito Acconci: Skatepark,* Institut Français d'Architecture, Paris

*Vito Acconci: High Rise of Models*,
Buildings Department, Munich

### 2001

*Vito Acconci: Performance Documentation and Photoworks,
1969–1973*, Ubu Gallery, New York

*Architecture Projects: Built, Unbuilt, Unbuildable, 1983–2001*,
ICAR Foundation, Paris

*Vito Acconci/Acconci Studio: Para-Cities*, Arnolfini Gallery,
Bristol, England*

## Group Exhibitions (since 1980)

### 1980

*Walls*, Contemporary Arts Center, Cincinnati

*Painting and Sculpture Today, 1980*, Indianapolis Museum of Art

*Morris, Acconci, Oppenheim,* Sonnabend Gallery, New York

*Hier et après / Yesterday and After*, Montreal Museum of Fine Arts*

*56 artistes + 1*, Centre d'Art Contemporain, Geneva*

*Festival of Two Worlds*, San Nicolo, Spoleto, Italy

*Drawings: The Pluralist Decade*, Biennale, Venice, Italy; Institute of Contemporary Art, University of Pennsylvania, Philadelphia*

*Dal Carpo al Nuovi Media Film / Performance*, Palazzo Reale, Teatro del Falcone, Genoa, Italy

*Biennale van de Kritiek*, International Cultureel Centrum, Antwerp, Belgium*

*A Sound Selection: Audio Works by Artists*, Artists Space, New York*

*Art of Conscience: The Last Decade*, Fine Arts Gallery, Wright State University, Dayton, Ohio

*Artist and Printer*, Walker Art Center, Minneapolis

### 1981

*1981 Biennial Exhibition*, Whitney Museum of American Art, New York*

*Westkunst: Zeitgenössische Kunst seit 1939*, Museen der Stadt Köln, Cologne*

*Video Classics*, Bronx Museum of the Arts, New York

*Variants: Drawings by Contemporary Sculptors*, Sewall Art Gallery, Rice University, Houston

*The Prison Show: Realities and Representation*, Whitney Museum of American Art Downtown at Federal Reserve Plaza, New York*

*The Kitchen Benefit Exhibition*, Paula Cooper Gallery, New York

*Soundings*, Neuberger Museum of Art, State University of New York, Purchase*

*Selections from the Chase Manhattan Bank Collection*, University Gallery, University of Massachusetts, Amherst*

*Radio by Artists*, A Space, Toronto

*Projects at the Precinct*, Creative Time, New York

*Other Realities: Installations for Performance*, Contemporary Arts Museum, Houston*

*Metaphor: New Projects by Contemporary Sculptors*, Hirshhorn Museum and Sculpture Garden, Washington, D.C.*

*Three Manifestos*, Lerner-Heller Gallery, New York

*Machineworks: Vito Acconci, Alice Aycock, Dennis Oppenheim*, Institute of Contemporary Art, University of Pennsylvania, Philadelphia*

*Italians and American Italians*, Crown Point Press, Oakland

*Home Made Movies: 20 Years of American 8mm and Super-8 Films*, Anthology Film Archives, New York*

*Films by American Artists: One Medium among Many*, Arts Council of Great Britain*

*Heart: A Collection of Artists' Books for Libraries, Museums, and Collectors*, Printed Matter, New York

*Art in Pursuit of a Smile*, Muhlenberg College, Allentown, Pennsylvania

*A Range of Contemporary Drawings,* Sordoni Art Gallery, Wilkes College, Wilkes-Barre, Pennsylvania

*Alternatives in Retrospect*, New Museum of Contemporary Art, New York

*Instruction Drawings: The Gilbert and Lisa Silverman Collection*, Cranbrook Art Museum, Bloomfield Hills, Michigan*

*In and Out of Kutztown: A Documentation of the Art Series Program, 1974–81*, Kutztown State College, Kutztown, Pennsylvania*

### 1982

*Documenta 7*, Museum Fridericianum, Kassel, Germany

*Tracking, Tracing, Marking, Pacing (Movement Drawings)*, Pratt Institute, Brooklyn*

*'60–'80: Attitudes / Concepts / Images*, Stedelijk Museum, Amsterdam*

*Record Covers for Show*, White Columns, New York

*Post-Minimalism*, Aldrich Museum of Contemporary Art, Ridgefield, Connecticut*

*Photographs in Painting and Sculpture*, Daniel Wolf, Inc., New York

*Photographs by Artists*, Galerie France Morin, Montreal

*Paintings and Sculpture by Candidates for Art Awards*, Art Galleries, American Academy of Arts and Letters, New York

*Octopus*, Museo del Barrio, New York

*New Directions: Contemporary Art from the Commodities Corporation Collection*, Museum of Art, Fort Lauderdale, Florida*

*National Video Festival*, American Film Institute, Los Angeles*

*Il pennello improprio*, Giardini de Bellariva, Florence

*Illegal America*, Exit Art, New York*

*Group Exhibition: Painting, Drawing, Sculpture, and Prints*, Paula Cooper Gallery, New York

*Four Manifestoes: Acconci / Baranik / Beuys / Mendieta*, Lerner-Heller Gallery, New York*

*Editions*, Gallery A, Amsterdam

*Drawings, Models, and Sculptures*, Fourteen Sculptors Gallery, New York

*Artists' Photographs*, Crown Point Press, Oakland*

*De la catastrophe*, Centre d'Art Contemporain, Geneva*

*Art and Dance*, Institute of Contemporary Art, Boston*

*Anti-Apocalypse: Artists Respond to the Nuclear Peril*, William Paterson College, Wayne, New Jersey

*Androgyny in Art*, Emily Lowe Gallery, Hofstra University, Hempstead, New York*

### 1983

*When Words Become Works*, Minneapolis College of Art and Design

*Urban Site*, 80 Langton Street, San Francisco

*Urban Pulses: The Artist and the City*, Pittsburgh Plan for Art*

*Sound / Art*, Sculpture Center, New York*

*Preparing for War*, Brooklyn Army Terminal

*1984*, Ronald Feldman Gallery, New York

*Minimalism to Expressionism*, Whitney Museum of American Art, New York

*Bridges*, Pratt Institute, Brooklyn

*Art Video: Retrospectives et Perspectives*, Palais des Beaux-Arts, Charleroi, Belgium*

*Art of Social Conscience*, Edith C. Blum Art Institute, Bard College, Annandale-on-Hudson, New York

### 1984

*Visions of Paradise: Installations by Vito Acconci, David Ireland, and James Surls*, Hayden Gallery, Massachusetts Institute of Technology, Cambridge*

*The Xmas Tree Show*, BACA Downtown, New York

*The Skowhegan Celebration Exhibition*, Hirschl & Adler Modern, New York

*Het lumineuze beeld / The Luminous Image*, Stedelijk Museum, Amsterdam*

*Staged / Stages*, Bernice Steinbaum Gallery, New York*

*Sound Art*, Sculpture Center, New York

*Soul Catchers*, Stellwig-Seguy Gallery, New York

*Selections from the Permanent Collection*, Museum of Contemporary Art, Chicago*

*Projects: World's Fairs, Waterfronts, Parks, and Plazas*, Rhona Hoffman Gallery, Chicago

*Outdoor Life*, The Red Studio, New York

*International Sculptural Invitational: Time and Space*, Visual Arts Center of Alaska, Anchorage*

*Hunger for Words*, Gallery 345, New York

*Furniture, Furnishings: Subject and Object*, Museum of Art, Rhode Island School of Design, Providence; Wesleyan University, Middletown, Connecticut; Munson-William-Proctor Institute, Utica, New York; Berkshire Museum, Pittsfield, Massachusetts; Vassar College of Art Gallery, Poughkeepsie, New York; Brattleboro Museum and Art Gallery, Brattleboro, New York; Maryland Institute College of Art, Baltimore*

*Etchings and Woodblocks*, Pace Editions, New York

*Ecritures dans la peinture*, Villa Arson, Nice, France*

*Drawings by Sculptors: Two Decades of Non-Objective Art in the Seagram Collection*, Montreal Museum of Fine Arts*

*Crown Point Pure Silk*, I. Magnin, San Francisco

*Contents: A Contemporary Focus, 1974–1984*, Hirshhorn Museum and Sculpture Garden, Washington, D.C.*

*Baubles*, Pratt Institute, New York

*Artists' Weapons: Peace and Good Will to All Men*, Ted Greenwald Gallery, New York

*Armed*, Interim Art, London

*The Last 80 Langton Street Catalogue*, New Langton Arts, San Francisco*

*1984 Visual Arts Program*, Artpark, Lewiston, New York*

### 1985

*Vème Biennale internationale de sculpture en plein air*, Skironio Museum Polychronopoulos, Athens

*Urban Artworks*, Public Art Space, Seattle

*37th Annual Purchase Exhibition*, American Academy of Arts and Letters, New York

*The Maximal Implications of the Minimal Line*, Edith C. Blum Art Institute, Bard College, Annandale-on-Hudson, New York*

*The Doll Show: Artists' Dolls and Figurines*, Hillwood Art Gallery, C. W. Post Campus, Long Island University, Greenvale, New York*

*The Bronx Celebrates*, Lehman College Art Gallery, City University of New York, Bronx*

*Ten: The First Decade*, University Gallery, University of Massachusetts, Amherst*

*State of the Art*, Twining Gallery, New York

*Promenades*, Parc Lullin, Centre d'Art Contemporain, Geneva*

*Process and Kunstruktion*, Künstlerwerkstatten, Munich*

*Mile-4*, Chicago Sculptural International

*Microcosms*, Maeght-Lelong Gallery, New York

*Memory Jam: A Retrospective of Films and Performances at Artists Space, 1974–1985*, Artists Space, New York

*Making Shelter*, Graduate School of Architecture and Design, Harvard University, Cambridge, Massachusetts

*Land / Space / Sculpture*, Addison Gallery of American Art, Phillips Academy, Andover, Massachusetts

*In Addition: Other Works by Artpark's 1985 Project Artist*, Buscaglia-Castellani Gallery, Niagara University, Niagara Falls, New York

*Houses*, Newhouse Gallery, Snug Harbor, New York

*Four Legs: The Dog Show*, Art Gallery at Harbor Front, Toronto

*Festival 85: Art Now*, University of North Carolina, Chapel Hill*

*Contemporary Art Auction to Benefit El Bohio*, El Bohio, New York

*Blossom Festival School Art Program*, Gallery, New School of Art, Kent State University, Kent, Ohio

*Biennale des Friedens*, Kunsthaus and Kunstverein, Hamburg*

*A Salute to the National Endowment for the Arts Twentieth Anniversary*, La Jolla Museum of Contemporary Art, La Jolla, California

Artpark, Lewiston, New York*

*Artists and Architects: Challenges in Collaboration*, Cleveland Center for Contemporary Art*

*Art and Time*, Palais des Beaux-Arts, Brussels

*Arresting Images*, 10 on 8, New York

*A New Beginning, 1968–1978*, Hudson River Museum, Yonkers, New York

*Adornments*, Bernice Steinbaum Gallery, New York*

### 1986

*Zugehend auf eine Biennale des Friedens*, Kunstverein and Kunsthaus, Hamburg

*Wienfluss 1986*, Vienna Festival*

*Vito Acconci, Nancy Dwyer, Matt Mullican,* 303 Gallery, New York

*Two Moon July*, The Kitchen, New York

*The Watermelon Show*, Gallery Hirondale, New York

*The Law and Order Show*, Barbara Gladstone Gallery, New York

*The First Decade*, Freedman Gallery, Albright College, Reading, Pennsylvania*

*The Fairy Tale: Politics, Desire, and Everyday Life*, Artists Space, New York

*The Doll Show*, Kilcawley Center Arts Gallery, Youngstown State University, Ohio*

*Single Shots: A Video History of Personal Expression*, Institute of Contemporary Art, Boston

*Sculpture: Acconci / Sherman / Steinbach / Wentworth*, Carpenter + Hochman Gallery, New York

*Public and Private: American Prints Today*, Brooklyn Museum*

*Place*, New Mexico State University, Las Cruces, New Mexico

*Picture This: Films Chosen by Artists*, Hallwalls, Buffalo

*Opening Exhibition*, Socrates Sculpture Park, Long Island City, New York

*1986: A Celebration of the Arts Apprenticeship Program*, City Gallery, New York

*New York City Video*, Artspace, Visual Arts Center, Surry Hills, Australia

*Intimate / Intimate*, Turman Gallery, Indiana State University, Terre Haute

*Engaging Objects*, Clocktower at P.S. 1 Contemporary Art Center, Long Island City, New York*

*Artists Support Black Liberation*, Galleria en El Bohio, New York

*Art in the Environment*, Boca Raton Museum of Art, Boca Raton, Florida*

*Ars Electronica*, Studio Oberösterreich, Linz, Austria*

*A.P.: Artists' Photographs*, Zona Archives, Florence

*An American Renaissance: Painting and Sculpture since 1940*, Museum of Art, Fort Lauderdale, Florida

*Real Time—Actual Space*, La Jolla Museum of Contemporary Art, La Jolla, California*

### 1987

*Prints in Parts,* Crown Point Press, New York

Acconci / Brenner / Gayman / Younger, American Fine Arts / Colin De Land Fine Arts, New York

*Perverted by Language*, Hillwood Art Gallery, C. W. Post Campus, Long Island University, Greenvale, New York*

*Concrete Crisis: Urban Images of the 80's*, Exit Art, New York

*The Success of Failure* (organized by Independent Curators Incorporated, New York), Laumeier Sculpture Park and Gallery, Saint Louis; Johnson Gallery, Middlebury College, Middlebury, Vermont; University of Arizona Museum of Art, Tucson*

### 1988

*Identity: Representations of the If*, Whitney Museum of American Art Downtown at Federal Reserve Plaza, New York

*International Landscape*, Galerie Christoph Durr, Munich

*The New Urban Landscape*, World Financial Center, New York

*The Debt*, Exit Art, New York

*Sculpture at the Point*, Point State Park, Pittsburgh*

*Private Works for Public Spaces*, R. D. Erpf Gallery, New York

### 1989

*Image World: Art and Media Culture*, Whitney Museum of American Art, New York*

*The Experience of Landscape: Three Decades of Sculpture*, Whitney Museum of American Art Downtown at Federal Reserve Plaza, New York*

*Immaterial Objects: Works from the Permanent Collection of the Whitney Museum of American Art*, North Carolina Museum of Art, Raleigh; Albany Museum of Art, Albany, Georgia; San Jose Museum of Art, San Jose, California; Whitney Museum of American Art at Equitable Center, New York*

*First Impressions: Early Prints by Forty-six Contemporary Artists*, Walker Art Center, Minneapolis*

*Contemporary Art from New York: The Collection of the Chase Manhattan Bank*, Yokohama Museum of Art, Yokohama, Japan*

*Une autre affaire*, Festival Nouvelles Scènes '89, Dijon, France

*China*, Asian American Arts Center, New York

*Recent Acquisitions*, Collett Art Gallery, Weber State College, Ogden, Utah

*International Landscape*, XPO Galerie, Hamburg*

*Taboo*, Greg Kucera Gallery, Seattle

### 1990

*Word as Image: American Art, 1960–1990*, Milwaukee Art Museum; Oklahoma City Arts Museum; Contemporary Arts Museum, Houston*

*Casino Fantasma*, Casino Municipale di Venezia, Venice, Italy*

*Conceptual Arts/ Conceptual Forms*, Galerie 1900/2000, Paris*

*Recent Print Acquisitions in Series*, Barbara Krakow Gallery, Boston

*Exposed*, Vivian Horan Fine Art, New York

*Selected Prints and Multiples*, Galerie Mai 36, Lucerne, Switzerland

*Pharmacy*, Jan Kesner Gallery, Los Angeles

*Assembled: Works of Art Using Photography as a Construction Element*, University Art Galleries, Wright State University, Dayton, Ohio*

*American Art Today: The City*, Art Museum at Florida International University, Miami*

*Hand, Body, House*, Barbara Shahn Galleries, William Paterson College of New Jersey, Wayne

*Concept-Décoratif: Anti-Formalist Art of the 70s*, Nahan Contemporary, New York*

### 1991

*1991 Biennial Exhibition*, Whitney Museum of American Art, New York

*Dissensi tra film video televisione*, Taormina Video Festival, Taormina, Italy*

*Power: Its Myths, Icons, and Structures in American Art, 1961–1991*, Indianapolis Museum of Art; Akron Museum of Art; Virginia Museum of Fine Arts, Richmond*

*The Fetish of Knowledge*, Real Art Ways, Hartford

*Departures: Photography, 1923–1990*
(organized by Independent Curators Incorporated, New York), Iris and B. Gerald Cantor Art Gallery, College of the Holy Cross, Worcester, Massachusetts; Denver Art Museum; Joslyn Art Museum, Omaha; Pittsburgh Center for the Arts; Goldie Paley Gallery, Moore College of Art, Philadelphia; Telfair Museum of Art, Savannah, Georgia*

*43rd Annual Academy Institute Purchase Program*, American Academy of Arts and Letters, New York

*Devices*, Josh Baer Gallery, New York

*True to Life*, 303 Gallery, New York

*Telekinesis*, Michner/Wilcox Gallery, San Francisco

*Poets/Painters Collaborations*, Brooke Alexander Editions, New York

*Video Library*, Andrea Rosen Gallery, New York

### 1992

*Allocations: Art for a Natural and Artificial Environment*, Floriade, Zoetermeer, Netherlands*

*The Power of the City / The City of Power*, Whitney Museum of American Art Downtown at Federal Reserve Plaza, New York*

*Environmental Terror: John Baldessari, Robert Fichter, Vito Acconci, Robert Morris, Hollis Sigler, Stuart Diamond, Katherine Porter, Fred Wilson, Maren Hassinger, Christy Rupp*, Fine Arts Gallery, University of Maryland; Stephanie Ann Roper Gallery, Frostburg State University, Frostburg, Maryland; East Main Street Gallery, Richmond, Virginia

*Functional Objects by Artists and Architects*, Rhona Hoffman Gallery, Chicago

*Surveillance*, Nancy Drysdale Gallery, Washington, D.C.

*Still*, Andrea Rosen Gallery, New York

*Animals*, Galerie Anne de Villepoix, Paris

*Habeas Corpus,* Stux Gallery, New York

*Tattoo*, Andrea Rosen Gallery, New York

*In through the Out Door*, Nordanstad/Skarstedt Gallery, New York

### 1993

*Vito Acconci, Bruce Nauman, Paul Thek*, Brooke Alexander Editions, New York

*5ᵉ Semaine internationale de vidéo*, Saint-Gervais, Geneva

*The Language of Art*, Kunsthalle, Vienna

*Contemporary Public Art in the Bronx*, Lehman College Art Gallery, New York

*Action / Performance and the Photograph*, Turner/Krull Galleries, Los Angeles*

*45th Annual Academy Purchase Exhibition*, American Academy of Arts and Letters, New York

*Second Tyne International*, Newcastle-upon-Tyne, England

*Photoplay: Works from the Chase Manhattan Collection*, Center for the Fine Arts, Miami*

*Abject Art: Repulsion and Desire in American Art*, Whitney Museum of American Art, New York*

*Il mondo del corpo*, Studio Oggetto, Milan

*Thresholds and Enclosures*, San Francisco Museum of Modern Art

*Live in Your Head*, Hochschule für Angewandte Kunst, Vienna

*Art and Application*, Turbulence, New York

### 1994

*Hors limites*, Centre Georges Pompidou, Paris

*The Ossuary*, Luhring Augustine, New York

*The Old Glory*, Cleveland Center for Contemporary Art*

*Tradition and Invention: Contemporary Artists Interpret the Japanese Garden*, Sogetsu Plaza, Sogetsu Kaikan, Japan*

*Outside the Frame: Performance and the Object*, Cleveland Center for Contemporary Art; Snug Harbor Cultural Center, Staten Island, New York*

### 1995

*Biennale d'art contemporain de Lyon*, Musée d'Art Contemporain de Lyon, France

*Ripples across the Water 95*, WATAR-IUM, Museum of Tokyo, Japan

*1965–1975: Reconsidering the Object of Art*, Museum of Contemporary Art at the Temporary Contemporary, Los Angeles*

*"Self Construction,"* Museum moderner Kunst, Stiftung Ludwig, 20er Haus, Vienna*

*Artists/Architects*, Nouveau Musée / Institut d'Art Contemporain de Villeurbanne, France

*Les années 80–90*, Musée d'Art Moderne, Villeneuve d'Ascq, France

*Landscape: A Concept*, California College of Arts and Crafts, Oakland

*Collisions*, Artekelu, San Sebastian, Spain

*Sculpture as Objects, 1915–1995*, Curt Marcus Gallery, New York

*Foundations: Underwear / Under Where?* Lawrence Gallery, Rosemont, Pennsylvania

*In a Different Light: Visual Culture, Sexual Identity, Queer Practice*, University Art Museum, Berkeley, California*

*ARS 95 Helsinki*, Museum of Contemporary Art, Helsinki*

*Temporarily Possessed: The Semi-Permanent Collection*, New Museum of Contemporary Art, New York*

### 1996

*L'art au corps: Le corps exposé de Man Ray à nos jours*, MAC—Galeries Contemporaines des Musées de Marseille, Marseilles, France*

*Biennale di Firenze*, Florence

*A History of Technological Visions since the Eighteenth Century*, Kunsthalle Wien, Vienna

*Sex and Crime: Von den Verhältnissen der Menschen*, Sprengel Museum, Hannover, Germany*

*NowHere*, Louisiana Museum of Modern Art, Humlebaek, Denmark

*Skin Deep: Works on Image, Body, Text*, Mercer Union, Toronto

*Retinal Circus*, Art Space, Copenhagen

*Art Chicago 1996*, Rhona Hoffman Gallery, Chicago

*Autoreverse*, Centre National d'Art Contemporain de Grenoble, France

*Passions privées: Collections particulières d'art moderne et contemporain en France*, Musée d'Art Moderne de la Ville de Paris, Paris*

*From Figure to Object*, Fifth Street Gallery, London

*A/drift: Scenes from the Penetrable Culture*, Center for Curatorial Studies, Bard College, Annandale-on-Hudson, New York*

*Photo-Works*, Brooke Alexander / Brooke Alexander Editions, New York

*Cause and Defect*, Spencer Brownstone Gallery, New York

*The Experimenters,* Lombard-Fried Fine Arts, New York

### 1997

*Broken Home*, Greene Naftali Gallery, New York

*In Site '97*, San Diego and Tijuana

*The Private Eye in Public Art*, Nations Bank Plaza, Charlotte, North Carolina

*Rooms with a View: Environments for Video*, Solomon R. Guggenheim Museum, New York

*Documenta X*, Kassel, Germany*

*Heaven*, P.S. 1 Contemporary Art Center, New York

### 1998

*Tracin'*, Ota Fine Arts, Tokyo, Japan

*Out of Actions: Between Performance and the Object, 1949–1979*, Museum of Contemporary Art, Los Angeles*

*Sculptors and Their Environments*, Pratt Institute, New York

*Conceptual Photography from the 60's and 70's*, David Zwirner Gallery, New York

*Voices*, Witte de With, Rotterdam; Fundació Joan Miró, Barcelona; Le Fresnoy, Studio national des arts contemporains, Tourcoing, France*

### 1999

*Seeing Time: Selections from the Pamela and Richard Kramlich Collection of Media Art*, San Francisco Museum of Modern Art*

*Comfort Zone: Furniture by Artists*, PaineWebber Art Gallery, New York

*People*, Andrea Rosen Gallery, New York

*Micro Space, Global Time: An Architectural Manifesto*, MAK Center for Art and Architecture, Los Angeles; MAK, Austrian Museum for Applied Arts, Vienna

### 2000

*The End: An Independent Vision of Contemporary Culture, 1982–2000*, Exit Art/The First World, New York

### 2001

*A Relationship Study, 1969–1976*, Galerie Lelong, New York

*Affecting Invention: The Manipulated Photograph*, Carrie Secrist Gallery, Chicago

# Selected Built Public Projects

Acconci Studio (Vito Acconci, Luis Vera, Jenny Schrider, Lisa Albin). *Wall of Ground,*
Arvada Art Center for the Arts and Humanities, 1992. Dirt, glass, galvanized steel. 24 x 352 x 4 ft.

**1983**

*House of Cars*, Langton Arts, San Francisco (temporary)

*See-Saw Bridge*, Pratt Institute, Brooklyn (temporary)

*Sub-Urb*, Artpark, Lewiston, New York (temporary)

*Way Station I (Study Chamber)*, Middlebury College, Middlebury, Vermont

**1984**

*Bad Dream House*, Massachusetts Institute of Technology, Cambridge (temporary)

*Face of the Earth*, Springfield, Massachusetts (temporary)

**1985**

*Bodies in the Park*, Parc Lullin, Geneva (temporary)

*House of Used Parts*, Harvard University, Cambridge (temporary)

**1986**

*House on the Ground*, New Mexico State University, Las Cruces, New Mexico

*Palladium Underground (Garden of Bodies)*, The Palladium, New York (temporary)

**1987**

*Displaced Personal Seating*, San Diego Museum of Contemporary Art, La Jolla, California

*Garden of Columns*, Coca Cola USA, Atlanta

**1988**

*Bad Dream House No. 2*, John Weiland Homes, Atlanta

*Birth of the Car/Birth of the Boat*, Three Rivers Festival, Pittsburgh (temporary)

*Face of the Earth No. 2*, C. W. Post College, Long Island University, Brookville, New York

*Face of the Earth No. 3*, Laumeier Sculpture Park, Saint Louis

*Garden with Fountain*, World Financial Center, New York (temporary)

*House of Cars No. 2*, Governor State College, Chicago

**1989**

*Floor Clock*, Equitable Building Plaza, Chicago
(reinstalled permanently at Chicago Dock and Canal in 1992)

**1991**

*Land of Boats*, St. Aubin Park, Detroit

*Mobile Linear City*, mobile unit, various locations, first
installed at Magasin, Grenoble, Switzerland

**1992**

*Wall of Ground,* Arvada Center for the Arts and Humanities,
Arvada, Colorado

*Personal Island*, Zoetermeer, Netherlands
(reinstalled permanently in Zwolle, Netherlands in 1994)

**1993**

*Personal River*, Tyne, Newcastle, England (temporary)

*Wall Machine*, Storefront for Art and Architecture, New York
(collaboration with Steven Holl)

**1994**

*Car Seating*, Tachikawa City, Japan

Ribbon for Embarcadero Promenade, San Francisco
(collaboration with Stanley Saitowitz and
Barbara Stauffer Solomon)

**1995**

*School on the Ground*, courtyard for P.S. 3, Bronx, New York

*More Balls for Klapper Hall*, Queens College, Queens, New York

Addition to MetroTech Gardens, MetroTech Center,
Brooklyn, New York

**1996**

*High Rise of Trees*, Atlanta (temporary)

*House up a Building*, portable unit,
first installed at Centro Gallego de Arte Contemporáneo,
Santiago de Compostela, Spain

*Park up a Building*, portable unit,
first installed at Centro Gallego de Arte Contemporáneo,
Santiago de Compostela, Spain

**1997**

Loloma Transportation Station, Scottsdale, Arizona
(collaboration with Douglas Sydnor and Angela Dye)

*Park in the Water*, The Hague, Netherlands

Walter Koenig's Bookstore, Documentahalle, *Documenta X*,
Kassel, Germany (temporary)

**1998**

*Flying Floors for Departures Terminal*,
Philadelphia International Airport, Philadelphia

*Walkways through the Wall,* Midwest Express Convention
Center, Milwaukee

**1999**

*Rooms from Below,* store windows for Saks Fifth Avenue,
New York (temporary)

**2000**

*Screens for a Walkway between Buildings and Buses and Cars*,
entrance to Shibuya subway station, Tokyo

*Courtyard in the Wind*, Buildings Department
Administration Building, Munich

**2001**

*Möbius Seating*, Fukuroi City, Japan

*Light Beams for the Sky of a Transfer Corridor*, San Francisco
International Airport, San Francisco

*Wall Slide*, seating system, 161st Street subway station,
Bronx, New York

# Writings by the Artist

## 1980

"(Here) …,""A Poster …,""A Store …,""(He Asked) …,"
"Page 1 …" [poems]. *Chelsea*, no. 39: 198–206.

"Notes on Work, 1969–1980." In *Vito Acconci:
A Retrospective, 1969–1980*. Exhibition catalogue. Chicago:
Museum of Contemporary Art.

"Now Do You Believe the Dirty Dogs Are Dead" [notes].
In *A Sound Selection: Audio Works by Artists*. Exhibition
catalogue. New York: Artists Space.

"The People Machine,""Let's Pretend This Is an Apparatus
for a Political Kidnapping,""Toward a Theory of Image:
Instrument/Decoration,""Movable Floor,""Decoy for Birds
and People" [notes]. *Cover*, no. 2 (January): 22–25.

"Situation Esthetics: Impermanent Art and the Seventies
Audience." *Artforum* 18 (January): 22.

"Some Grounds for Art as a Political Model" [notes].
In *Art of Conscience: The Last Decade*. Exhibition catalogue.
Dayton: Fine Arts Gallery, Wright State University.

"V.D. Lives/ T.V. Must Die" [notes and audiotape transcript].
*Journal (Los Angeles Institute of Contemporary Art)*
(February–March): 21–28.

## 1981

"American Pop" [notes]. *Zone* (spring–summer): 9–11.

"Combination,""Command Performance" [notes].
In *112 Workshop, 112 Greene Street: History, Artists, and
Artworks*, edited by Robyn Brentano with Mark Savitt,
132–33. New York: New York University Press.

"Mobile Home" [notes]. *Benzene* (summer–fall): 26.

## 1982

"Biography of Work 1969–1981,""Abstract House" [notes].
In *Documenta 7*. Exhibition catalogue. Kassel: Museum
Fridericianum. Vol. 1: 174–76; vol. 2: 4–5.

"Exploding House" [notes]. *Rampike* 2, no. 3: 24–25.

"High Rise,""Instant House,""Mobile Home" [notes].
*Perspecta: Yale Architecture Journal*, no. 18: 100–107.

"Notes on Drawing." In *Tracking, Tracing, Marking, Pacing*.
Exhibition catalogue. Brooklyn: Pratt Institute.

"Now Do You Believe the Dirty Dogs Are Dead" [audiotape].
*Live to Air*. Magazine of cassette tapes. London.

Recorded documentation of notebook entries for exhibition
and commission, San Diego State University, California
(April–May 1982).

"Some Notes on Illegality in Art." In *Illegal America*.
Exhibition catalogue. New York: Exit Art.

## 1983

"Devices for Guards and Prisoners" [notes]. *Rampike* 3,
no. 1: 12–13.

"Sub-Urb" [notes]. In *1983 Visual Arts Catalog*.
Exhibition catalogue. Lewiston: Artpark.

"Ten-Point Plan for Video,""Contacts,""Face-Off,""Claim"
[notes]. In *Kunst und Video*, edited by Bettina Gruber and
Maria Vedder, 72–75. Cologne: Dumont Buchverlag.

"Three Columns for America" [notes]. In *Sound/Art*.
Exhibition catalogue. New York: Sculpture Center.

"Vito Acconci" [edited lecture transcript],
in "Site: The Meaning of Place in Art and Architecture."
*Design Quarterly* (summer): 4–5.

## 1984

"Four Story Table" [notes]. In *International Sculptural
Invitational: Time and Space*. Exhibition catalogue.
Anchorage: Visual Arts Center of Alaska.

"House of Cars" [notes]. *Rampike* 3, no. 4: 4–6.

"Notebook: On Activity and Performance." In *The Art of
Performance: A Critical Anthology*, edited by Gregory
Battcock and Robert Nickas, 194–98. New York: E. P. Dutton.

"Some Notes on Visions of Paradise." In *Visions of Paradise:
Installations by Vito Acconci, David Ireland, and James Surls*.
Exhibition catalogue. Cambridge: Hayden Gallery,
Massachusetts Institute of Technology.

"Televisions, Furniture, and Sculpture: The Room with the
American View,""Body Capsule" [notes]. In *Het lumineuze
beeld / The Luminous Image*. Exhibition catalogue.
Amsterdam: Stedelijk Museum.

## 1985

"Bad Dream House,""Bridge Chairs for Sex and Gender,"
"Face of the Earth" [notes]. In *Alles und noch viel mehr: Das
poetische ABC*, edited by G. J. Lischka, 575–77. Bern: Benteli.

"Bodies in the Park" [notes]. In *1985 Visual Arts Program*.
Exhibition catalogue. Geneva: Parc Lullin, Centre d'Art
Contemporain.

"Instant House" [notes]. *Rampike* 4, no. 2–3: 30–31.

"Notes on Collaboration." In *Artists and Architects: Challenged in Collaboration*. Exhibition catalogue. Cleveland: Cleveland Center for Contemporary Art.

"Notes on Line." In *The Maximal Implications of the Minimal Line*. Exhibition catalogue. Annadale-on-Hudson: Edith C. Blum Art Institute, Bard College.

"On Growing Up in the Bronx." In *The Bronx Celebrates*. Exhibition catalogue. Bronx: Lehman College Art Gallery, City University of New York.

"Playing with the Word 'Dolls.'" In *The Doll Show: Artists' Dolls and Figurines*. Exhibition catalogue. Greenvale, N.Y.: Hillwood Art Gallery, C. W. Post Campus, Long Island University.

"Security Zone" [notes]. In *Technicians of the Sacred*, edited by Jerome Rothenberg, 571–18. Berkeley: University of California Press.

"Some Notes toward a Theory of Public-Space Art." In *Mile 4*. Exhibition catalogue. Chicago: Chicago Sculpture International.

### 1986

"Biography" [notes]. In *The Arties: Franklin Furnace's Tenth Anniversary Album*. New York: Franklin Furnace.

"Homebodies (An Introduction to My Work 1984–5)." In *Vito Acconci: The House and Furnishings as a Social Metaphor*. Exhibition catalogue. Tampa: USF Art Galleries, University of South Florida.

"Notes on Vienna and on a Piece for the Vienna Festival." In *Wienfluss 1986*. Exhibition catalogue. Vienna: Vienna Festival.

"Some Notes on the Phantom of the Paradise." In *Picture This: Films Chosen by Artists*. Exhibition catalogue. Buffalo: Hallwalls.

Untitled teaching assignments. In *Sketchbook with Voices,* edited by Eric Fischl with Jerry Saltz. New York: Alfred van der Marck Editions.

### 1987

"Normal Art: Art in Public Places." In *Vito Acconci: Domestic Trappings*, by Ronald J. Onorato, 61–68. La Jolla, Calif.: La Jolla Museum of Contemporary Art.

"Notes on Language." In *Perverted by Language*. Exhibition catalogue. Greenvale, N.Y.: Hillwood Art Gallery, C. W. Post Campus, Long Island University.

"Notes on the Failure of 'Machine for Living.'" In *The Success of Failure*. Exhibition catalogue. New York: Independent Curators Incorporated.

"A Possible Model for Fairy Tales." *New Observations* 45 (1987): 12–13.

### 1988

"Coming Out (Notes on Public Art)." In *Vito Acconci: Public Places*, by Linda Shearer, 20–31. New York: Museum of Modern Art.

"Notes on My Photographs, 1969–1970" and "Notebook Excerpts, 1969." In *Vito Acconci: Photographic Works, 1969–1970*. New York: Brooke Alexander Inc.

"Projects of Home." *Artforum* 26 (March): 126–28.

### 1989

"Notes on Making Shelter." *Harvard Architecture Review* 7: 35.

### 1990

"Public Space in a Private Time." *Critical Inquiry* 16 (summer): 900–918.

### 1991

Untitled text in "(Why) Is David Lynch Important?" *Parkett* (June): 159.

### 1992

"The *Bárriadas* as a Model for Public Art." In *Allocations: Art for a Natural and Artificial Environment*, edited by Jan Brand, Catelijne de Muynck, and Jouke Kleerebezem, 204–5. The Hague and Zoetermeer: Foundation World Horticultural Exhibition Floriade.

"Bodies of Land." *Blauwe Kamer*, no. 3 (June): 34–37.

"Frames for Life." *Art and Text* (May): 82–87.

"Performance after the Fact." *Documents (sur l' Art Contemporain)* (March): 44–50.

### 1993

"Making Public: The Writing and Reading of Public Space." In *Vito Acconci: Making Public*. The Hague: Stroom Haags Centrum Voor Beeldende Kust.

### 1995

"Parks, Streets, and Vehicles." *Grand Street*, no. 54 (fall): 24–33.

### 2000

"Words before Music" (unpublished).

# Bibliography

**Monographs**

*Please note that exhibition catalogues are listed in the exhibition history.*

Linker, Kate. *Vito Acconci*. New York: Rizzoli, 1994.

Moure, Gloria, ed. *Vito Acconci: Writings, Works, Projects*. Barcelona: Ediciones Polígrafa, 2001.

**Selected Periodical Articles**

### 1980

Auer, James. "Acconci Talks About a Revolution That Failed." *Milwaukee Journal*, 27 April.

Bonesteel, Michael. "Art and the Occult." *New Art Examiner* 8 (November): 1.

Burnham, Jack. "Acconci in a Tight Spot: Interview with Vito Acconci." *New Art Examiner* 7 (May): 1, 8–11.

Celant, Germano. "Dirty Acconci." *Artforum* 19 (November): 76–83.

Cox, Meg. "A Conceptual Artist Deals with Everything from Bugs to Jeers." *Wall Street Journal*, 25 April.

Jordan, James. "A Critic Reveal(ed)(ing)." *Dialogue* 3 (November–December): 4–5.

Kirshner, Judith Russi. "Interview with Vito Acconci." *Interview* 10, no. 5.

Kunz, Martin. "The Development of Physical Action into a Psychic Intensity of the Picture." *Flash Art*, no. 98–99 (summer): 12.

Kuspit, Donald. "Art of Conscience: The Last Decade." *Dialogue* 3 (September–October): 19–21.

Loughran, Catherine. "Two Artists' Horoscopes: An Astrological Blindfold Test." *New Art Examiner* 8 (November): 11.

Morgan, Stuart. "Vito Acconci, The Kitchen; Vito Acconci, Robert Morris, Dennis Oppenheim, Sonnabend Gallery." *Artforum* 18 (summer): 82–83.

"Vito Acconci: The Body Impolitic." *Art in America* 68 (October): 118–23.

Stevens, Mark. "Vito Acconci: The Art of Shocking." *Newsweek*, 28 April, 95.

### 1981

Avigos, Jan. "Interview with Vito Acconci." *Art Papers* 5 (January–February): 1–5.

Foster, Hal. "Review: Vito Acconci at Max Protetch." *Artforum* 20 (October): 75.

Harvey, Donald. "An Interview with Vito Acconci." *Dialogue* 3 (January–February): 54–57.

Kahl, Susie. "Performance Recorded through Installation Site." *Artweek* 12 (September 19): 1.

Lawson, Thomas. "1981 Whitney Biennial." *Flash Art*, no. 103 (summer): 42.

Linker, Kate. "Review: Metaphors, New Projects by Contemporary Sculptors." *Artforum* 20 (March): 73.

Morgan, Stuart. "Review: 'Machineworks,' Institute of Contemporary Art." *Artforum* 20 (summer): 97–98.

Morris, Robert. "American Quartet." *Art in America* 69 (December): 91–105.

Platt, Susan. "Vito Acconci: The Sheltering City." *Artweek* 12 (4 September): 1.

Russell, John. "Open Storage Spaces." *New York Times*, 8 January, sec. C.

Schwartz, Ellen. "Vito Acconci: 'I Want to Put the Viewer on Shaky Ground.'" *Art News* 80 (summer): 93–99.

Taylor, Paul. "Self as Theatricality: Samuel Beckett and Vito Acconci." *Art and Text* (autumn): 2–11.

### 1983

Curtis, Cathy. "City Sites." *Artweek* 14 (17 September): 5.

McEvilley, Thomas. "Art in the Dark." *Artforum* 21 (summer): 62–71.

Olejarz, Harold. "Bridges." *Arts Magazine* 58 (September): 17.

### 1984

Cohen, Ronny. "Jumbo Prints: Artists Who Paint Big Want to Print Big." *Art News* 83 (October): 87.

Foster, Hal. "For a Concept of the Political in Art." *Art in America* 72 (April): 17–25.

Glueck, Grace. "Staged/Stages." *New York Times*, 21 December, sec. C.

Raynor, Vivien. "Explanations for 'Success of Failure.'" *New York Times*, 21 December, sec. C.

Regen, David, and Kevin Noble. "Public Address: 'Sign on a Truck.'" *Art in America* 72 (January): 91.

Rice, Shelly. "The Luminous Image: Video Installations at the Stedelijk Museum." *Afterimage* 12 (December).

Van Wagner, Judy K. Collischen. "Sound Art." *Arts Magazine* 59 (September): 19.

### 1985

"Album: Vito Acconci." *Arts Magazine* 59 (February).

Brenson, Michael. "What's New around Town in Outdoor Sculpture." *New York Times*, 19 July, sec. C.

Cone, Michele. "Vito Acconci at Carpenter + Hochman." *Flash Art*, no. 122 (April–May): 38–39.

Freedman, Samuel G. "Vietnam in America: The War and the Arts." *New York Times Magazine*, 21 March, 50–56.

Greenberg, Blue. "Vito Acconci: The State of the Art, 1985." *Arts Magazine* 59 (June–summer): 120–23.

Goodman, N. "Vito Acconci at Rhona Hoffman Gallery." *New Art Examiner* 13 (April): 54.

Hornsfield, Kate. "On Art and Artists: Interview with Vito Acconci." *Profile* 4, no. 3–4.

Linker, Kate. "Vito Acconci at Carpenter + Hochman." *Artforum* 24 (May): 113–14.

Marter, Joan. Artpark: Site Installations in Retrospect." *Arts Magazine* 59 (January): 132–34.

McEvilley, Thomas. "I Think, Therefore I Art." *Artforum* 24 (summer): 74–84.

Philips, Patricia C. "Vito Acconci." *Artforum* 24 (March): 114.

"Vito Acconci at Nature Morte." *Artforum* 24 (February): 89–90.

"Vito Acconci: Nature Morte Gallery." *Arts Magazine* 59 (January): 36.

Wechsler, Max. "Paradise Regained." *Artforum* 25 (September): 94–97.

### 1987

Brenson, Michael. "Sculpture That Springs from Surrealism." *New York Times*, 8 March, sec. 2.

Freudenheim, Susan. "Port Art: Give Peace a Chance." *San Diego Tribune*, 29 May, sec. D.

Hinson, Mark. "Interview with Vito Acconci." *Art Papers* 11 (March–April): 41–42.

Knight, Christopher. "An Artist Shapes His Private World in Public Spaces." *Los Angeles Herald Examiner*, 12 July, sec. F.

Levin, Kim. "Vito Acconci at International with Monument." *Village Voice*, 17 March, 86.

Phillips, Patricia C. "Vito Acconci at International with Monument." *Artforum* 25 (summer): 121.

Pincus, Robert. "Acconci's Art No Stranger to Controversy." *San Diego Union*, 8 June, sec. D.

Rochette, Anne, and Wade Saunders. "Vito Acconci at International with Monument." *Art in America* 75 (June): 150.

### 1988

Casorari, Cecilia. "Vito Acconci." *Contemporanea* 1 (September–October): 107.

Gimelson, Deborah. "The Fourth Dimension." *Art and Auction* 10 (May): 170–79.

Goldberger, Paul. "Winter Garden Party at Battery Park City." *New York Times*, 12 October, sec. C.

Kimball, Roger. "Is MoMA Attempting Suicide?" *New Criterion* 6 (April): 30–38.

Kimmelman, Michael. "A Tamer Vito Acconci Show at the Modern." *New York Times*, 19 February, sec. C.

Kuspit, Donald. "Vito Acconci: The Hunger Artist in a Lonely Crowd." *Artscribe* 70 (summer): 64–67.

Larson, Kay. "Art: Changing of the Avant-garde." *New York*, 29 February, 124–26.

Levin, Kim. "Vito Acconci: Public Places." *Village Voice*, 8 March, 54.

Princethal, Nancy. "Vito Acconci." *Sculpture* 7 (May–June): 12–15.

Small, Michael. "Vito Acconci: Put Him on Exhibit but Don't Say 'Don't Touch.'" *People*, 31 October, 78–82.

### 1989

Jones, Bill. "Vito Acconci." *Arts Magazine* 63 (summer): 77.

Levin, Kim. "Vito Acconci." *Village Voice*, 21 March, 40.

Liu, Catherine. "Erotophobia—Simon Watson Gallery." *Artforum* 28 (October): 176–77.

Rian, Jeffrey. "Past Sense, Present Sense." *Artscribe* 73 (January): 60.

Schjeldahl, Peter. "La Dolce Vito." *Seven Days*, 22 March, 63–64.

Schwartzman, Allan. "Monumental Trouble." *Elle*, September, 298.

Taubin, Amy. "Video and Language." *Village Voice*, 19 September, 49.

Woodward, Richard B. "Documenting an Outbreak of Self-Preservation." *New York Times*, 22 January, sec. 2.

### 1990

Humphrey, David. "Vito Acconci at James Corcoran." *Art Issues*, no. 13 (September–October): 28–29.

Kimmelman, Michael. "Venice Biennale Opens with Surprises." *New York Times*, 28 May, sec. C.

Marks, Ben. "An Irresistible Pairing: Vito Acconci at James Corcoran Gallery." *Artweek* 21 (21 June): 17–18.

Pejic, Bojana. "Art ex Absentia." *Artforum* 28 (April): 144–50.

Weissman, Benjamin. "Vito Acconci—James Corcoran Gallery." *Artforum* 29 (October): 177–78.

Wilson, William. "Vito Acconci's Massive Sculptures Turn to Thoughts of Home." *Los Angeles Times*, 12 June, sec. F.

### 1991

Gardner, Paul. "New York Wrap-up: Vito Acconci." *Art News* 90 (September): 78–79.

Hirsch, Faye. "Vito Acconci." *Arts Magazine* 65 (summer): 77.

Homes, A. M. "Vito Acconci—Barbara Gladstone Gallery." *Artforum* 29 (summer): 107.

Larson, Kay. "Mixed Messages." *New York*, 15 April, 69.

McEvilley, Thomas. "Two Big Shows: Post Modernism and Its Discontents—New York: The Whitney Biennial." *Artforum* 29 (summer): 98–101.

Princethal, Nancy. "Keeping Abreast." *Art in America* 79 (July): 108–11.

Schor, Mira. "You Can't Leave Home without It." *Artforum* 30 (October): 114–19.

### 1992

Bonami, Francesco. "Vito Acconci" (interview). *Flash Art* (Italy), no. 166 (February–March 1992): 86–88.

Casadio, Maricchia. "Vito Acconci: When Art Becomes Architecture." *Interview*, January, 32.

Fleck, Robert. "Vito Acconci: Body Trap." *Flash Art* 25 (March–April): 104.

Heartney, Eleanor. "Skeptics in Utopia." *Art in America* 80 (July): 76–81.

Hirsch, Faye. "France in Review." *Arts Magazine* 66 (January): 94–95.

Kremer, Mark. "Vito Acconci—Magasin, Grenoble." *Artscribe* 90 (February–March): 91.

Nesbitt, Lois. "The Young, The Wild, and the Wicked: Art's Bad Boys." *Elle*, March, 130–32.

### 1993

D'Amato, Brian. "Vito Acconci/303 Gallery." *Flash Art* 26 (May–June): 84–85 (ill.).

Flood, Richard. "Rosebud, Anyone? (Artist's Favorite Films)." *Frieze*, no. 9 (March–April): 35.

Geveres, Ine. "Vito Acconci." *Metropolis*, no. 3 (March): 41.

Hughes, David. "Making Do: The Work of Vito Acconci." *Hybrid*, no. 4 (August–September 1993): 6–9.

Melrod, George. "Studio: Vito Acconci." *Sculpture* 12 (March–April): 10–11.

"A Museum Piece, Vienna." *Domus*, no. 753 (October): 1–3.

Rian, Jeff. "What's All This Body Art?" *Flash Art* 26 (January–February): 50–53.

Schreiner, Wolfgang. "Vito Acconci: The City inside Us." *Vernissage* (February): 41–43.

### 1994

Phillips, Patricia C. "Vito Acconci and Steven Holl." *Artforum* 32 (March): 90–91.

Rian, Jeff. "I Never Wanted to be Political: I Wanted the Work to *Be* Politics" [interview]. *Flash Art* 27 (January–February): 84–87.

Smith, Stephen K. "Vito Acconci." *Forum* 19 (March): 3.

Thorson, Alice. "Artist Finds Provocation Part of His Mission." *Kansas City Star*, 20 February.

"Vito Acconci: Projects, Pier 18 at the Kunstverein." *Flash Art* 27 (March–April): 52.

### 1995

Czoppan, Gabi. "Künstler des Jahres." *Focus*, no. 43 (October): 120–23.

Larson, Kay. "Artists Are the Directors, and a Stage Is Their Canvas." *New York Times*, 8 October.

Van de Walle, Mark. "Vito Acconci—Dia Center for the Arts." *Artforum* 33 (December): 88.

**1996**

Brea, José Luis. "Vito Acconci—Centro Galego de Arte Contemporanea." *Artforum* 34 (September): 117.

Linda, Maria, and Sina Najafi. "Vito Acconci." *Index* (January): 24–27.

**1997**

"The Electronic Gallery." *New York Times Magazine* ("What Technology Is Doing to Us: A Special Issue"), 28 September, 59.

Heartney, Eleanor. "Report from Japan: 'Art: Live and in Public.'" *Art in America* (March): 50–55.

Lutticken, Sven. "Zeepsop, poes en hellende schots." *Parool*, 9 December, 13.

Ruzicka, Joseph. "Lines to Be Filled In Later: An Interview with Vito Acconci." *On Paper* 1 (July–August 1997): 26–30.

Smith, Roberta. "A Channel-Surfing Experience with Beanbag Chairs and Gym." *New York Times*, 25 April, sec. C.

**1998**

Ayers, Robert. "Out of Actions." *Art Monthly*, no. 214 (March): 214–17.

Griffin, Tim. "Vito Acconci, 'Spoken Rooms (3 Installations, 1974–75).'" *Time Out*, 26 March.

Kool-Want, Christopher. "Vito Acconci: Video and Performance." *Contemporary Visual Arts*, no. 18.

Mariño, Melanie. "Vito Acconci at Barbara Gladstone." *Art in America* 86 (November).

Obrist, Hans Ulrich. "Unbuilt Roads." *Contemporary Visual Arts*, no. 20: 36–38.

"Tele-Furni-System." *ID Magazine: Forty-fourth Annual Design Review* 45 (July–August): 164.

**1999**

"Flying Floors, Philadelphia International Airport." *ID Magazine: Forty-fifth Annual Design Review* 46 (July–August): 172.

Getter, Tamara. "Vito Acconci: A Conversation with Tamara Getter." *Studio* (November): 27–37.

Nobel, Philip. "As Always, Please Touch." *New York Times*, 8 April, sec. D.

Parola, Lisa, "Acconci Studio: Viafarini a Milano Ospita Il Body Artista." *Stampa,* 12 April, 17.

Shultz, Heinz. "Vito Acconci: Die Bedeutung von Offentlichkeit." *Kunstforum*, no. 144 (March–April): 286–95.

Volk, Gregory. "The Carnivalized Sublime." *Daidalos*, no. 73 (September): 68–77.

**2000**

Bayliss, Sarah "Inside, Outside, Upside Down." *Art News* 99 (April): 150–53.

Bennett, Paul. "Methane Dreams." *Landscape Architecture* 90 (March): 20.

Celant, Germano. "Corpo a corpo d'autore." *Espresso*, 17 August, 153.

Frazer, Ward. "The Space around the Corner: A Conversation with Vito Acconci." *Documents* 19 (fall): 67–79.

Paparoni, Demetrio. "Vito Acconci." *Tema celeste*, no. 78 (March–April): 56–63.

Teyssot, Georges. "Public Spaces and the Public Agora." *Lotus International*, no. 107 (September): 68–77.

"Tidal Bridge." *Landforum* 6 (October): 109.

**2001**

Gellatly, Andrew. "Still Life in Mobile Homes." *Frieze*, no. 58 (April): 75–79.

Ho, Cathy Lang. "Curriculum Vito" [interview]. *Architecture* 90 (January): 51–54.

Rush, Michael, "Before 'Reality TV' There Was Reality Video." *New York Times*, 21 January, sec. 2.

"Situations/Interchanges." *Lotus International*, no. 108 (March): 66–75.